Pulpit of Leaves:
Deception in Plain Sight

*Unmasking Counterfeit Voices,
Charisma, and Control in the Church*

Justin & Kasey Greenwell

the-unchurched.org

CUMBEES HOUSE OF PUBLISHING

CUMBEES HOUSE of Publishing

A Wholly Owned Subsidiary of CUMBEES HOUSE
Whiteville NC 28472 Office: (910) 300-7700
www.cumbees.com email: tv@cumbees.com

ISBN: 978-1-971163-03-1 (Hardback)
ISBN: 979-8-9930517-6-5 (Paperback)
ISBN: 978-1-971163-20-8 (Paperback)
ISBN: 978-1-971163-00-0 (eBook)
ISBN: 978-1-971163-04-8 (Audio)
Library of Congress Control Number: 2025926301

Printed in the United States of America
10 9 8 7 6 5 4 3 2 1

This book contains personal reflections, recollections,
and opinions of the authors. Names, identifying details,
and certain events have been changed or withheld to
protect privacy. Any resemblance to actual persons,
living or dead, is coincidental and not intended by the
authors.

Table of Contents

Chapters

Our Next Book is Coming Soon!
***UNCHURCHED:** Coming Out of Corrupt Systems and Returning to the True Body of Christ*

Scan the QR code below to find out more

Bible Copyright Notices

Disclaimer

This book is a work of personal testimony and spiritual reflection based on the experiences, perceptions, and recollections of the authors within various ministry settings. It is written for healing, edification, and faith-based discussion and reflects the authors' understanding of events at the time they occurred.

To protect the privacy of individuals, churches, and communities, identifying details have been altered, generalized, combined, or omitted and some individuals or events may be presented as composite portrayals. Certain accounts have been paraphrased or condensed to preserve confidentiality while conveying the intended spiritual reflections.

The views expressed are those of the authors alone and are presented as personal opinion and experience, not as verified fact, legal conclusion, or accusation. This work is not investigative reporting and does not assert criminal or civil liability. Its purpose is not to defame or harm but to encourage reflection, healing, accountability, and growth within the Body of Christ, pointing readers toward truth and restoration in Jesus Christ.

Repentance

Father, I repent to You for every time I sinned and confused Your work with the work of man, every moment I accepted applause when conviction should have been rising in my heart, and the times I mistook favor for blessing and power for presence. I repent for allowing silence to feel more comfortable than truth, standing still when I should have spoken, and accepting money, influence, or approval that did not come from You. I repent for every time I saw something that grieved Your heart and justified it instead of confronting it. I repent for calling what was convenient *"unity"* when it was really fear.

Forgive me, Lord, for failing to protect Your sheep the way You protected me. You entrusted me with souls and I protected systems. You called me to shepherd, but I settled for surviving. Mercy found me and it did not leave me where it found me.

To the Reader, I repent to you for any way my silence, complicity, or misplaced loyalty may have misrepresented Christ to you, the moments I held titles instead of holding space for honesty, every time I chose peace in the room over peace with God, every meeting where I stayed quiet when truth was on trial, and every time my obedience to man made it harder for you to believe in the goodness of God. I repent for the years I spent excusing what I should have exposed and every time I confused submission with surrender and unity with uniformity. If my silence strengthened spiritual abuse, then my repentance must strengthen your freedom. It has taken time, tears, and truth to face what I was a part of, but grace met me at every step. God has not only forgiven me, but He has also freed me. Through that freedom, He taught me something I will never forget: **"Loyalty to man will always cost you the clarity of God, but loyalty to God will always bring you closer to truth and to freedom."** *"Let your conversation be without covetousness; and be content with such things as ye have: for He hath said, I will never leave thee, nor forsake thee"* **(Hebrews 13:5 KJV).** I don't need to buy favor, a platform to be heard, or a ministry to be a son. I have Jesus and He is enough. The Lord took every illusion of strength I had built and broke it. It was not to destroy me but to restore me and not to rob me of calling but to return me to the heart of it. Now I know I want nothing to do with what looks like revival but smells like pride. I want everything to do with what looks like humility and leads to Jesus.

Dedication

This book is dedicated to the Body of Christ, the true
Church, not built by human hands but formed by the
Spirit of the Living God. I write to those who hunger
for truth beyond tradition, who still listen for the gentle
voice of the Spirit, and who are willing to choose
obedience even when it is costly. Real love tells the
truth and healing begins with humility. Restoration does
not start with accusation but with the courage to admit
where we have fallen short and to return together back
to the Father. Writing this book has cost me more than I
can express. It has not been written in anger, betrayal,
or rebellion but in prayer, tears, and obedience. My
prayer is that these words are received with open hearts
and not hardened defenses. I offer them not to wound or
divide but to heal and restore. I share this book with
love, honor, and with a deep longing to see God's
people walk again in humility, honesty, and a life that
truly reflects Jesus. May this be received as an
invitation to truth, healing, and restoration within the
Body of Christ.

A Call to Prepare Your Heart

As we begin walking through the journey of what we
have experienced as staff pastors in a high-profile
ministry from 2021 to 2025, we ask that you understand
the heart behind this book. This is not a book of
exposure or retaliation. We will not recount our
experiences in a way that directs hearts against any
specific church or ministry. This book has been written
under direct instruction from the Lord God, Yehovah.
We recognize that Jesus himself spoke clearly of
ministries and leaders that would arise in the world. He
gave us wisdom and spiritual insight to discern between
those who bear the fruit of the Spirit and those who do
not. His words were not meant to sow suspicion but to
safeguard the purity of His Church.

It is under this divine understanding that we have been
led by the Lord to create this work. God has mandated
us to lead this effort and bring together like-minded
believers who are called to help others come out from
among environments of religious abuse within the
church. This book serves as a personal account of what
we have experienced as staff pastors. We will not
fabricate our stories, nor will we exaggerate them. We
will share what we have lived truthfully, transparently,
and with the intent to bring understanding and healing
to others.

We write to help you understand *why* this book exists.
It is not born of offense but of obedience. We pray that
through these pages many will find confirmation of
what they have discerned, comfort in knowing they are
not alone, and clarity to separate truth from deception.
We pray that this work will validate countless believers
who have left ministries under the confusion of control,
as well as those currently sensing heightened spiritual

discernment and seeking the Lord for further understanding.

This is an account of our experience within a high-profile church ministry. However, this is not a blanket statement against the Body of Christ as a whole. We fully acknowledge and deeply honor the many wonderful, spirit led, and Christ centered churches across America. We write not to condemn the church but to help her bring awareness, healing, and biblical discernment to a generation that is witnessing both the greatest outpouring and the greatest deception of our time.

We pray that this book helps congregants, ministry leaders, and those who have suffered religious abuse to see with renewed clarity what is actually taking place in many churches after the lights go out on stage in these last days.

The Mindset of the Staff

Before you judge anything written in these pages, wonder how anyone could stay, or ask yourself, *"Why did they not speak up sooner?"* you must understand the mindset every staff member lived in when this story began. We were not skeptics or rebels, nor were we wounded wanderers looking for power or position. We were lovers of Jesus, servants hungry for revival, and a couple who would have given their last breath to see one soul come to Christ. We came with clean hands, pure hearts, and an unshakable belief that God himself had planted us there. We prayed for the broken until our voices cracked, held strangers as they wept in our arms, and stood in the gap for families, marriages, addicts, and prodigals. We gave everything and we gave it willingly. Our story begins here because our hearts were open and our trust was complete. Our desire to please God was so fierce we did not see the gradual shift happening around us, at least not at first. It was gentle, subtle, wrapped in Scripture, disguised as honor, unity, loyalty, and a spiritual covering. What we later recognized as manipulation first looked like commitment. What was actually control felt like discipleship and fear felt like reverence but later would be exposed as abuse. In the beginning it looked like personal sacrifice.

We were conditioned through spiritual language, verbal threats, emotional and financial dependency, and disciplinary actions that would be enforced if not compliant with their demands. The environment taught us that asking questions was dishonor, setting boundaries was rebellion, discomfort meant our hearts were not right, discernment was suspicion, exhaustion was something to repent for, and silence was spiritual maturity. Our spirits whispered, *"Something is wrong...*" but the culture around us thundered, *"Submit. Obey. Trust. Die to yourself."* So, we did. We laid ourselves on altars that we were never meant to die on. None of us endured this because we were weak. We endured it because we were devoted, loved God more than we loved ourselves, and believed we were giving Him our obedience rather than surrendering our identities. The very qualities that made us good servants such as compassion, loyalty, humility, and self sacrifice became the qualities that were weaponized against us. This is not written to excuse what we tolerated. It is written to reveal how easily spiritual abuse can clothe itself in righteousness and how even the strongest believers can lose themselves when the language of God is used to justify the actions of man. By the time the cracks became undeniable, we had already been shaped by an emotional, psychological, and spiritual system that taught us to reinterpret every red flag as a lack of faith. We were not blind, we were conditioned. Instead of being indifferent, we were overwhelmed. We were not complicit, but we were drowning in expectations we believed came from God himself. So, before you read another word, understand this: **This could happen to any leader, believer, or person whose heart burns for the things of God.** We were not foolish; we were faithful. That is exactly why it took us so long to see the truth.

This story is not just about what happened. It is about **how** it happened and how easily the purest hearts can be reshaped in an environment that confuses the voice of leadership with the voice of the Lord. Read these pages with compassion and discernment knowing that behind every moment of silence was someone who believed they were doing the will of God. Only then will the gravity of what we endured and what we escaped, fully come into view.

Leaders Say, *"This Is Not True"*

There may be leaders that are sincere and will publicly say that the things written in this book are not true. Before anyone absorbs those words or allows them to create doubt, I want to gently explain something that is absolute essential to understand: **Our former pastors would only allow us to associate with their approved pastors and congregants.** These leaders only saw the public version, polished presence, spiritual language, and stage persona. They did not see the private moments that shaped this book. They have not:

- sat where we sat
- endured what we endured in staff meetings
- been behind closed doors where manipulation, pressure, and emotional control took place
- heard the words that made us question ourselves or doubt our own discernment
- held the phone and read the text messages we were sent
- been in the meetings where promises were made and broken
- experienced the spiritual weight, confusion, or internal battles we woke up to every single day

So, when a leader, especially one who is *not* part of this staff life, steps forward to defend, deny, or excuse what is written here, please understand they:

- are not withholding the truth; they simply do not possess it.
- cannot speak about conversations they were never invited into.
- cannot testify about behavior they have never witnessed.
- cannot validate or refute experiences they never lived.

These leaders are responding from the place of relationship they *do* have, a relationship crafted through the lens the pastors gave them, but they do not know them the way we were required to know them. They were never entrusted with the weight of their private expectations, demands, and corrections. They were not present for the moments that reshaped, challenged, and in many cases wounded us. Their loyalty was real, but it was loyalty built on partial access, not full truth. So, if you hear a leader say, *"None of this ever happened,"* or *"This is exaggerated,"* or *"This is false,"* I ask you to consider the more honest question: **How could they know?** They were not there and did not live the day-to-day reality of ministry behind the curtain. They only walked in the light that was permitted to shine in their direction.

This is not written to shame them but to protect you from confusion. Their perspective was limited to what our former pastors wanted them to see, not because the leaders outside the church are dishonest, but because their access was carefully managed. They knew the public shepherds, not the private wolves.

This book exists to:

- pull back what was hidden
- give voice to what was silenced
- honor the truth that only those in the inner rooms ever truly experienced

We write this not out of anger but out of clarity: **"Do not let the words of those who never saw or heard the truth convince you to ignore those who lived in it."**

The Biblical Foundation

"Beware of false prophets, which come to you in sheep's clothing, but inwardly they are ravening wolves. Ye shall know them by their fruits. Do men gather grapes of thorns, or figs of thistles? Even so every good tree bringeth forth good fruit; but a corrupt tree bringeth forth evil fruit. A good tree cannot bring forth evil fruit, neither can a corrupt tree bring forth good fruit. Every tree that bringeth not forth good fruit is hewn down, and cast into the fire. Wherefore by their fruits ye shall know them" **(Matthew 7:15–20 KJV)**.

This passage was given to believers as a standard of discernment so that we might recognize the difference between those who truly walk in the Spirit and those who merely perform works in His name.

Any pastor can preach a powerful sermon. Anyone can stand behind a pulpit and declare fervent prayers over a congregation. Men and women can prophesy, operate in deliverance, and even witness miracles in the context of their church. Yet the fruit Jesus referred to in this passage is not found in gifted preaching, prophetic ability, or public ministry. **The fruit Jesus seeks is the fruit of the Spirit: the character, humility, integrity, and holiness that flow from a life surrendered to Him.**

It is possible for pastors to present the illusion of fruitful ministry while privately living lives that contradict the very message they proclaim. Many trees appear lush and covered in leaves, yet when inspected closely, they bear no fruit. Leaves create the image of life, but fruit proves it. The true measure of a minister is not found in their public gifting but in their private obedience. *"But the fruit of the Spirit is love, joy, peace, long-suffering, gentleness, goodness, faith,*

Meekness, temperance: against such there is no law"
(*Galatians 5:22–23* KJV).

If a leader's life does not reflect what they preach, their actions will inevitably speak louder than their words. The way a pastor treats people, manages authority, and handles responsibility behind closed doors will testify far louder than any microphone ever could.

In these last days, Jesus warned that false prophets would arise, clothed in humility and holiness on the outside but inwardly motivated by pride, power, and control. They would look like shepherds but devour like wolves. I did not go searching for such a wolf, but I did fall victim to one. In finding one, we have come to fully understand why the Lord brought us to this ministry. It was to testify not to tear down but to call God's people to truth, healing, and holiness once more.

Introduction

We must come to terms with a sobering truth. A wolf in sheep's clothing is rarely revealed at first glance. Deception in the church is often subtle, creeping in through familiarity, charisma, or even what appears to be bold truth. As Jesus warned us, *"Beware of false prophets, which come to you in sheep's clothing, but inwardly they are ravening wolves"* **(Matthew 7:15 KJV).** Many believers will live years under such deception before the scales finally fall from their eyes.

Our story is a testimony of that very phenomenon. It did not begin with suspicion or distrust but quite the opposite. If you had told us just a few years ago that we would be writing this book, exposing what we have seen and endured, we would not have believed you. We were initially captivated by what appeared to be a ministry of boldness and uncompromising faith. For six full months, my wife and I watched every live stream, astonished by the authority in the preaching. The wolf's firm stance on COVID-19 mandates and sound biblical expositions resonated deeply within us. We admired the church's proclaimed generosity and outward zeal for the things of God. We were so aligned with the message being preached that we made a bold decision. We packed up our three children, then ages one, three, and nine and drove three and a half hours every Sunday to attend in person.

June 2021 marked our first time on campus. The atmosphere was electric. It portrayed charisma, crowds, and the fire. I'd never seen anything like it in all my years of church experience. Through this ministry's

17

preaching, God did a mighty work in us. We were still straddling the world, but the *Word* began to take root and transform us. For that, I remain grateful. *"For the word of God is quick, and powerful, and sharper than any twoedged sword..."* **(Hebrews 4:12 KJV)**. Indeed, that Word pierced our hearts.

Soon, we were convinced the Lord was leading us to do more. Through much prayer and petition, we decided to sell our home. We fixed it up, put it on the market, and in November 2021, we became Tennessee residents, fully immersed in the culture of the church. We were at every prayer meeting, event, and volunteer opportunity. If the church needed something, we were there.

One night, my wife was in prayer as she looked at the chaos overtaking the ministry's online pages filled with negativity and spam. God gave her a full, strategic outline to help. We made an appointment with the wolf, thinking we would simply offer our help. At this point, we had only spoken to him once before, in a meet and greet line. To our surprise, this appointment turned into a job offer. We were invited to join the staff. It was one of the greatest days of my life, or so I thought. Yet as Scripture reminds us, *"...man looketh on the outward appearance, but the LORD looketh on the heart"* **(1 Samuel 16:7 KJV)**. Little did we know that everything we saw on the outside was not as it appeared on the inside. My wife and I would go on to become the longest standing pastors on staff. We served in multiple seasons, working with thousands of people through various ministry efforts. I will never deny that good things happened during that time. Miracles, salvations, and powerful moves of God took place. However, as this book will reveal there were also red flags, flags we did not recognize while walking through them. We were spiritually immature when we began. We had only been walking in full surrender to the Lord for approximately a year. Much of what we saw felt *"off,"* yet we suppressed our concerns. I questioned myself instead of questioning leadership and I doubted my own discernment rather than the behavior I witnessed. I watched too many times, members being treated in ways no human should endure, especially not in the Body of Christ. I experienced things that I never expected to see in ministry, behaviors I know now were neither biblical nor holy. The Apostle Paul warned the church: *"For such are false apostles, deceitful workers, transforming themselves into the apostles of Christ"* **(2 Corinthians 11:13 KJV)**. Yet in my immaturity and misplaced trust, I often failed to recognize this.

It was not until November 2025, that God in His mercy fully removed the scales from my eyes. Like Saul on the road to Damascus, I had my own moment of awakening. This book is not just a record of what others have done; it is also an honest account of my own shortcomings: *"Confess your faults one to another, and pray one for another, that ye may be healed"* **(James 5:16 KJV)**. I am committed to transparency because as a wise woman once said, *"Transparency disarms the enemy."* I have been mandated by God to expose what grieves His heart and to help heal what has been wounded in His church.

As you read, you will see places where I failed and did not speak up when I knew something was wrong. I take full responsibility for that. I allowed spiritual manipulation to quieten me for far too long. For that, I deeply repent before the Lord and before you, my brothers and sisters.

This book was birthed through intense prayer. Every page has come through hours of reflection, repentance, and pleading with God. You will not just read our experiences, but you will see from Scripture what God has to say about every topic we address. This is not about exposing people but revealing the truth. We understand this is not just about us but about the Church of the Living God: *"For the time is come that judgment must begin at the house of God..."* **(1 Peter 4:17 KJV)**.

A Symptom of a Deeper Sickness

The ministry we sat under was not the problem. It was a symptom of a much bigger disease. What we have experienced is not confined to one building, pulpit, or leadership team. It is part of a deeper sickness that has spread quietly through portions of the modern church. When accountability is replaced with loyalty, authority is centralized without plurality. When questioning is labeled rebellion and spiritual language is used to silence pain, the issue is no longer local but systemic. These patterns repeat themselves across congregations, denominations, and movements, often excused in the name of unity, anointing, or protection of *"the work of God."* Scripture warned us this would happen. Paul cautioned that wolves would arise not only from outside the flock but from among its own leaders, men speaking twisted things to draw disciples after themselves. Jesus rebuked religious systems that looked righteous on the outside while rotting within, calling them whitewashed tombs. They were beautiful in appearance but full of death beneath the surface. The danger was never just individual failure; it was a culture that learned how to excuse, defend, and spiritualize it.

Our story is one expression of a much larger crisis in the Body of Christ. It is a crisis of unchecked power, celebrity driven leadership, fear-based obedience, and control masquerading as spiritual authority. It is a system that protects platforms over people, image over integrity, and leaders over the wounded. Dismissing this as *"just one church"* is to miss the invitation God is extending to His people. We must examine what we have normalized, defended, and have been too afraid to confront.

This is not written to tear down the church but to call her back to health. Scripture tells us that judgement begins in the house of God, not as condemnation but as loving correction. The church does not need better branding, stronger marketing, or louder platforms. She needs repentance, humility and leaders who tremble at the Word of God more than they protect their own influence. This is not about one house of worship but about the condition of the entire Body of Christ.

Healing will not begin until we are willing to admit what we are seeing is not an anomaly; it is a warning.

Chapter 1
Spiritual Leadership and Authority

Test All Things: Not Blindly Follow

"Prove all things; hold fast that which is good" (**1 Thessalonians 5:21 KJV**). The Apostle Paul gives a timeless and essential command to the church: *"Prove all things."* The word **prove** here means to test, examine, and discern. This is not a suggestion but a responsibility. Blind acceptance has no place in the house of God. In the context of spiritual leadership, this Scripture has immediate relevance. God never intended for His people to follow any man unquestioningly, even if that man has authority, charisma, or even a reputation of power. The Gospel frees us from the bondage of blind allegiance and calls us into spiritual maturity that discerns truth from error, even when error comes wrapped in religious language.

The Biblical Standard for Leadership

True biblical leadership is not defined by how many people follow without question but by how faithfully the leader aligns with Scripture. Leaders are called to be shepherds, not dictators. Here's what the Bible says about leaders who reflect Christ like authority: *"Neither as being lords over God's heritage, but being examples to the flock"* (**1 Peter 5:3 KJV**). Leaders are to be examples, not tyrants.

Genuine authority in God's kingdom is humble, accountable, and rooted in Christ's nature. Leaders are not the final authority, God is: *"...We ought to obey God rather than men"* (**Acts 5:29 KJV**). Any system that demands obedience to man at the expense of obedience

22

to God is spiritually twisted. Blind loyalty corrupts both leader and follower. God calls His people to be wise, discerning, and spiritually alert. Failure to test what is being said or commanded, opens the door for manipulation, deception, and abuse. A pastor who demands loyalty rather than earning respect has already stepped outside of biblical boundaries.

Why Testing Is Critical in Ministry

Some ministries today operate in direct opposition to *1 Thessalonians 5:21*. Instead of encouraging spiritual discernment, they rely on the emotional loyalty of their people. They discourage questions, call dissent rebellion, and equate disagreement with disloyalty, but Scripture says the exact opposite. The Bereans were commended for searching the Scriptures. Even after hearing from Paul himself *"...they received the word with all readiness of mind, and searched the scriptures daily, whether those things were so"* **(Acts 7:11 KJV)**. If the Apostle Paul encouraged examination of his teaching, what makes any modern leader exempt? Pastors who demand unquestioned loyalty, whether through emotional pressure or implied spiritual consequence, are not biblically aligned. They are undermining the very nature of the Gospel, where the Holy Spirit leads believers into truth, not leaders who insist on control.

Testing a leader's words and actions is not rebellion, it is obedience to God. When Scripture says, *"hold fast that which is good,"* it implies that some things are not good, even when coming from someone in authority. To *"prove all things"* is not a lack of faith; it is the exercise of Godly wisdom. The Holy Spirit never asks you to discard your discernment at the door of the sanctuary. The biblical foundation has been laid knowing that God calls us to test all things, including spiritual leadership. I want to invite you into a deeply personal chapter of my life. This is not easy to share; I do so with great reverence for the Lord and the truth of His Word.

Silence Rather than Truth

As I look back over the years my family and I spent serving in this ministry, I can now see what I could not then. If I had truly understood Paul's warning in *1 Thessalonians 5:21* *"Prove all things; hold fast that which is good"* I might have spared myself and my family, much confusion, misplaced loyalty, and heartbreak. I wish I could tell you that I noticed the *red flags* immediately and discerned the difference between godly authority and human control, but the truth is, I did not. Like so many others, I was drawn to what looked like the power of God. I saw passion, boldness, and conviction. These things on the surface mirrored revival. I was hungry for truth and believed I had found it. We weren't rebellious or bitter. We were simply eager to give God our everything including time, talents, resources, and our hearts. I have learned that loyalty without biblical discernment can easily become deception dressed in devotion.

At first our service came from sincerity, but slowly the atmosphere began to change. Serving was not just encouraged; it became demanded. Honor was no longer a posture of the heart; it was a requirement of the system. The expectation was not just faithfulness; it was unquestioned submission, even when Scripture was contradicted.

Here's where I must take responsibility. I saw things that did not sit right, heard words that pricked my spirit, and watched decisions that did not align with the Word of God. Yet, I stayed silent. I told myself that questioning would be disloyal and speaking up might *"hurt the church."* I questioned whether I was just not spiritually mature enough to understand, but in truth, I was afraid of losing position, favor, and belonging. I convinced myself that silence was submission when it really was self-preservation. When truth is on the line, silence is harmful. I share this now not to point fingers but to lift the mirror and show you what can happen when sincere believers mistake loyalty for holiness and silence for humility. I was one of them and have repented deeply before the Lord for every moment I chose peace with man over truth before God.

Conviction Meets Control

When my wife and I joined the pastoral team in 2022, there was a faithful couple already serving in leadership. We will call them *Phil and Linda*. Phil led the men's ministry and Linda co-led the women's ministry alongside the wolf's wife, the false prophetess. The couple were respected, gentle, sincere, and deeply committed to the people of the church. Over time, they began noticing troubling patterns within the staff. There were issues that did not align with biblical order or integrity. Following the clear instruction of **Matthew 18:15**, Phil privately approached the wolf voicing his concerns with humility and care. He shared that the Lord had also shown him that one day he would step into his own ministry and that God would make the timing clear. Instead of being heard, he was dismissed. His discernment was framed as disloyalty. The issues continued and the atmosphere worsened.

Then one Wednesday night without warning, the wolf called Phil and others out publicly from the pulpit for expressing concerns about another staff member. In that moment, what had been handled privately was weaponized publicly. Phil knew then that the Lord was closing one season and opening another. He submitted

25

his letter of resignation explaining that God was calling him into a new season of ministry. The wolf refused to accept it and attempted to convince him to stay but Phil was resolved. He obeyed what the Lord had placed on his heart and stepped away. Phil and Linda quietly left choosing conviction over comfort. At the time, I told myself they must have been out of order. I repeated the phrases that I had heard, they were *"offended, deceived, and caused division."* I did not seek the truth for myself, go to them, or defend them. I simply accepted the narrative because it was easier and safer.

After their departure, Phil and Linda began a small ministry rooted in family, discipleship, and healing. This was exactly what Phil had said the Lord was calling him to do. Instead of being blessed and released, they were discredited. Rumors spread that they were *"starting a ministry off the backs of the church."* To the staff, the wolf claimed they had lied and even implied they had stolen. Staff were explicitly told not to contact them. I was warned that doing so could cost me my job. So, I stayed silent and I regret it to this day. Instead of handling the matter with grace and protecting them as family, we exposed it with gossip and treated them as enemies. About a year later, the very staff member Phil had raised concerns about resigned under serious conflict. Phil and Linda's warnings were proven right. Yet no apology was ever made; their reputations remained stained. I cannot rewrite that history, but I can confess my part in it. I stayed silent when I should have spoken. I feared man more than I feared God.

Stewardship Loses Accountability

In 2024 another pastor, let's call him *Allen*, began asking questions, this time about finances. Our church had raised nearly $2 million for a building purchase. When the sale fell through many of us assumed the funds were being stewarded toward a new location but shortly after the wolf and false prophetess purchased a $1.6 million home in the church's name. They furnished it lavishly, bought two new vehicles, and even gifted cars to others.

In the pulpit the wolf often said, *"Anyone who wants to see the books can see the books."* Allen took him at his word. When he asked to see them, he was denied. I was present along with my wife Kasey, the wolf, and another church member during a meeting that the wolf held with Allen. During that conversation the wolf openly admitted that there was **no official board** and that he had *final say over all financial decisions*. He said he was accountable only to *"friends in ministry"* outside the church. We later learned that despite statements of the church previously dissolving its 501(c)(3) status, that the organization still appeared as active in public records. This raised serious concerns for us about whether the ministry was still operating under nonprofit requirements. Allen raised these concerns respectfully and we agreed privately that the situation was troubling and potentially improper. We expressed our discomfort and asked for clarification. We were assured that the matter would be addressed. In the meeting, the wolf would not tell us the identity of the *"businessmen"* who supposedly donated the $1.6 million for the home which was put in the church's name after the purchase of the new church fell through. According to the phone calls that I answered for the church, the wolf borrowed hundreds of thousands of dollars from congregants online in the form of *"loans"* for the new church that was never purchased. We asked to see the books and were denied. We inquired about spending decisions, museum purchases, extravagant travel, and unexplained expenses but did not receive clear or direct answers. We also asked who reconciled

27

the books at the end of each tax year and the response
was the wolf's wife handled it. We asked who held the
wolf accountable within the church and the answer was
simply, no one. This does not demonstrate biblical
leadership, humility, or the fear of the Lord.
The early church was built on shared authority, mutual
submission, and transparent stewardship. No pastor is
exempt from that. No leader stands above
accountability. I remember walking away from that
meeting torn. I knew what was right, but I convinced
myself it was not my place to say more. I told myself
that God would deal with it. While that may sound
spiritual, it was really fear disguised as faith. I see that
now. **James 4:17 KJV** says, *"Therefore to him that
knoweth to do good, and doeth it not, to him it is sin."*
That verse disturbs me in the most holy way. I was not
malicious, but I was passive. I did not gossip, but I did
not guard. While I did not contribute to the harm, I did
not help stop it either. This is why I write now, not as a
judge but as a witness and not to expose but to exhort.
What I have shared is not a tale of villains and victims.
It is the story of believers, me included, who lost sight
of truth while trying to protect what we loved. My
silence was my greatest regret, but it has now become
my greatest teacher. I learned that standing for truth is
not rebellion. Loyalty to man must never come before
loyalty to God. Now with repentance and renewed
conviction, I tell this story not to destroy but to deliver.
If my failure can help someone else find courage to
"prove all things" and hold fast to what is good, then
the years I spent silent will not have been wasted.
Together we will step into what happened next. Paul
warns us: *"Providing for honest things, not only in the
sight of the Lord, but also in the sight of men"* **(2
Corinthians 8:21 KJV)**. Financial transparency is not
optional, it's biblical.

Loyalty is Twisted and Truth is Punished

As the months passed, I began to see more clearly what once blurred together as *"honor"* and *"unity."* Behind the scenes things continued to unfold in ways that I now recognize were far from healthy. At that time, I rationalized, ignored, or quietly justified their actions in the name of loyalty and submission. When questions about finances began to surface, the wolf persuaded a trusted congregant, the Jester, to befriend Allen. Allen believed this man was a friend and confided in him, sharing his heart, concerns, and prayers. What Allen did not realize was that these conversations were being reported back to the wolf. Private trust became weaponized information. Though it grieved me, I stayed quiet. I saw enough to feel uneasy but did not have enough courage to stand against it. Allen handled the entire situation with far more integrity than I did. When he realized he could no longer stay in good conscience, he chose to resign. Immediately, the narrative shifted. He was accused of stealing $30,000, though no proof was ever presented. His name, calling, and reputation were dragged through the mud. In the pulpit, he was painted as disloyal, deceptive, and spiritually unstable. No one on staff was given clarity or allowed to ask questions. Once again, I stayed silent.

A message came through our staff group thread a few weeks after Allen had stepped away and started his own church. It was a voice memo from the wolf's wife. Her tone was calm, almost gentle but her words cut deep. She said something along the lines of this, *"If anyone feels the need to look at the books, you're free to do so. But understand you will no longer be employed here because the need to see the books shows me you don't trust your leadership."* The thread went silent. Not one person replied. I remember staring at that message, my heart pounding, realizing what had just been said.

Transparency had officially been labeled as betrayal and accountability as rebellion. The invitation to *"trust leadership"* now meant *"don't ask questions."* Still, I said nothing. I wish I could say that I stood up that day, pushed back, and found my voice. I did not because I was afraid. I had children to provide for, bills to pay, and a home that the ministry itself had helped me get into. I felt trapped spiritually, financially, and emotionally. The truth is, I did not see a way out without costing my family everything.

So, I stayed silent. I justified my fear as wisdom and told myself I was protecting my family, when in reality I was only prolonging the pain. That was the day I finally began to see what the Lord had been trying to show me all along. When access is treated as accusation and truth is treated as disloyalty, integrity has already been replaced by control. *"For every one that doeth evil hateth the light, neither cometh to the light, lest his deeds should be reproved"* (**John 3:20 KJV**). It was a sobering revelation, one that forced me to wrestle with the cost of truth. Would I continue to call silence loyalty? Or would I finally follow truth, even if it cost me everything? This moment in early 2025 sparked a new chapter within me. One where I began to plan my exodus.

Looking back, I can see how fear disguised itself as honor in my heart. I told myself that God would handle everything. If I said something it might cause division, but division was already there. It was just dressed in the language of *"order"* and *"obedience."* What was truly dividing the body was not telling the truth but silencing it. *"...Touch not mine anointed, and do my prophets no harm"* (**Psalm 105:15 KJV**). This verse was quoted often to protect leadership from accountability. However, the harm being done was not to those in authority, it was to the flock beneath them. The same Scripture meant to guard the anointed was being used to shield misconduct. Now I understand how dangerous that is. To this day, I have no connection with *Phil and Linda* or *Allen* because leadership demanded separation, not reconciliation. We were told distance was wisdom, but in truth it was control. I complied. That realization has been one of my deepest sources of repentance before God. Now I understand any church culture that suppresses questions, punishes dissent, and isolates truth-tellers is not operating under the Spirit of Christ. It is not just unhealthy, it's unbiblical. *"For where envying and strife is, there is confusion and every evil work"* (*James 3:16* KJV). The Spirit of God does not exist where there is confusion, control, or fear.

Truth Makes You a Target

Over time it became heartbreakingly common to watch brothers and sisters in Christ suffer for simply asking questions. Many were called divisive, rebellious, or worse. One couple stands out vividly in my memory. They were a gentle, sincere family, and devoted to the life of the church. They requested a meeting with the wolf to discuss what they believed the Lord had shown them, areas of sin that needed repentance. They came privately, humbly, and following **Matthew 18:15** hoping to appeal in love. Instead of being heard, they were dismissed and discredited. In the pulpit, the wolf publicly mocked their conversation saying, *"If I were in that much sin, I'd resign immediately."* The couple left quietly while being wounded, grieving, and branded as divisive. They were not the only ones.

I witnessed others attempt to bring correction in love, only to be humiliated, called rebellious, or labeled as witches. I remember people standing during services desperate, emotional, pleading for the wolf to repent, only to be forcibly removed by in-house security in

31

front of the entire congregation. It was a surreal thing to watch. On the surface, it was presented as *"order being restored."* In my spirit, it felt like something holy was being quenched. The warning from **Galatians 4:16** echoed in my heart: *"Am I therefore become your enemy, because I tell you the truth?"* The more I watched, the more I began to realize that questioning leadership was not rebellion but righteousness. Unfortunately, at that time I did not have the courage to say it. The wolf frequently said, *"If you don't agree with your leadership, then leave. Someone else will take your seat next week."* He considered his arrogance confidence, but it created a culture of fear. It was a place where disagreement meant exile.

There were so many stories like this, countless families who left, and countless private meetings that ended in pain. For the sake of time, I can only share a few. However, each one left a mark on me and planted a question in my heart that I could no longer ignore.

The Call to Question

The unraveling of blind loyalty did not happen overnight. It came slowly and painfully like light breaking through a thick fog. The Lord began to deal with my heart before He ever dealt with the culture around me. He showed me that questioning authority, when done with humility and love, is not rebellion. It's responsibility. I had been conditioned to equate silence with unity. Silence in the face of sin is not unity, it's complicity. What I had once called loyalty, God exposed as fear of being:

- rejected
- misunderstood
- cast out

But then the Word of God began to come alive in me again: *"There is no fear in love; but perfect love casteth out fear..."* (*1 John 4:18* KJV). The love of God began to teach me that questions, when asked from a pure heart, are not rebellion but reverence. They are a form of accountability. They are how the Body of Christ protects itself from deception. The Lord gently reminded me that even Jesus, at twelve years old, sat among the teachers in the temple *asking questions* (*Luke 2:46* KJV). If the Son of God could inquire, discern, and challenge understanding surely His followers could too. So, I began to change. Not all at once, but in small, surrendered steps. I began to speak when prompted, question when convicted, and listen to the voice of the Holy Spirit above the voice of fear. It was here in that holy breaking, that my eyes began to open. For the first time in years, I began to see what true spiritual health looks like. It is not control or intimidation but love, truth, and light. That is where this journey now leads.

Questions Are a Form of Accountability

The same Paul who wrote, *"Obey them that have the rule over you..."* (*Hebrews 13:17* KJV) also told believers to *"STAND fast therefore in the liberty wherewith Christ hath made us free..."* (*Galatians 5:1* KJV). God is not the author of confusion or oppression. Asking questions in the church when something seems off does not break unity; it protects it. Scripture is filled with examples of righteous questioning:

- **Nathan questioned King David** after his sin with Bathsheba (*2 Samuel 12* KJV).
- **Paul confronted Peter** for his hypocrisy (*Galatians 2:11-14* KJV).

- **The Bereans questioned Paul's teaching**, searching the Scriptures daily to confirm truth (*Acts 17:10-11* KJV).

They were not viewed as rebellious but as noble: *"These were more noble than those in Thessalonica, in that they received the word with all readiness of mind, and searched the scriptures daily, whether those things were so"* (*Acts 17:11* KJV). I realized if God allows His Word and even His apostles to be examined, what makes a pastor exempt from being questioned? My duty as a staff pastor was to shepherd, *Not Silence*. I remained silent out of loyalty to my leaders, but the Lord convicted me for that silence, showing me that it was not true loyalty; it was a failure to be faithful to the truth. *"CRY aloud, spare not, lift up thy voice like a trumpet, and shew my people their transgression..."* (*Isaiah 58:1* KJV).

Blind Loyalty, Broken

When blind loyalty dies, true growth begins. I began to live in spaces where truth mattered more than titles, accountability mattered more than applause, and integrity replaced intimidation. In that place, God began to rebuild me, not as a *"yes man"* but as a true shepherd. The kind of shepherd who:

- guards the flock not only from outside wolves but from wolves in the fold
- loves God's people enough to risk being misunderstood
- understands that pastoral authority is not about control, it's about responsibility

Blind loyalty stunts growth, but biblical discernment leads to maturity: *"But strong meat belongeth to them that are of full age, even those who by reason of use have their senses exercised to discern both good and evil"* **(Hebrews 5:14 KJV)**. Discernment is not automatic; it is learned, sharpened, and activated when we stop surrendering our spiritual judgment at the altar of personality. Now I know it is not only my right to question when something is wrong but also my duty as a pastor, believer, and a child of God.

Healing from Spiritual Authority

Wounds inflicted by spiritual leadership cut deeper than most because they strike at the place where trust was meant to be safest. When authority is misused in the name of God, it does not just confuse the mind, it fractures the soul. Scripture never denies this reality. In fact, it names it plainly. God rebukes shepherds who feed themselves instead of the flock and declares that He Himself will require His sheep at their hand **(Ezekiel 34:2-10 KJV)**. Healing begins when we stop pretending that all authority is automatically holy, simply because it carries a title. Many believers walked away from abusive spiritual leadership feeling disoriented, guilty, or afraid. They were taught that questioning leadership was rebellion, disagreement was pride, and leaving was abandonment of God's will. However, the Bible never equates spiritual maturity with silence. Discernment is not dishonor; it is obedience to truth. True spiritual authority exists to serve, not to dominate. Jesus was explicit: *"...Ye know that the princes of the Gentiles exercise dominion over them... But it shall not be so among you..."* **(Matthew 20:25-26 KJV)**. When leadership demands unquestioned loyalty, suppresses conscience, or equates itself with God's voice, it has crossed from shepherding into control. Healing requires acknowledging that misuse of authority is not your failure, it is a violation of God's design.

One of the most damaging effects of spiritual abuse is the distortion of God's character. Leaders may have spoken for God in ways that were rooted in fear, insecurity, or self-preservation. Over time, people begin to associate God with threat instead of love. Scripture draws a sharp line between God and abusive authority: *"The LORD is righteous in all his ways, and holy in all his works"* **(Psalm 145:17 KJV)**. If something was manipulative, coercive, or shaming, it did not reflect His character, no matter how spiritual it sounded. Healing also involves releasing false guilt. Many carry shame for staying too long but Jesus never condemned wounded sheep for being deceived. He rebuked the leaders who caused them to stumble and warned that it would be better for such leaders to have a millstone tied around their neck than to harm one of His little ones **(Matthew 18:6 KJV)**. Your survival is not disobedience; it is evidence of God's mercy.

Restoring a healthy understanding of authority takes time. Scripture teaches that all human authority is limited and accountable. Even apostles submitted themselves to the judgment of the church and to one another **(Galatians 2:11–14 KJV)**. No leader in the Scriptures was beyond correction. Healing comes when believers relearn that loyalty belongs to Christ first, not to an institution, personality, or platform: *"...one is your Master, even Christ; and all ye are brethren"* **(Matthew 23:8 KJV)**.

As trust is rebuilt, God gently restores discernment. *"My sheep hear my voice..."* **(John 10:27 KJV)** does not mean sheep never get confused; it means the Shepherd remains faithful to call them back. The goal of healing is not to make you suspicious of all leadership but to make you anchored in truth so that leadership is tested, not feared or idolized. Scripture encourages this balance: *"Obey them that have the rule over you..."* **(Hebrews 13:17 KJV)** is always held in tension with *"...We ought to obey God rather than men"* **(Acts 5:29 KJV)**.

Ultimately, healing from wounded authority comes through encountering Jesus as He truly is:

- He does not manipulate.
- He does not coerce.
- He does not threaten compliance.
- He invites.
- He leads by example.
- He lays down His life for the sheep (*John 10:11* KJV).
- He restores it where leadership took life.
- He heals where authority crushed.
- His perfect love casts out fear where it once ruled (*1 John 4:18* KJV)

Healing is not forgetting what happened; it is learning to trust God again without surrendering your conscience to man. It is allowing the Chief Shepherd to reteach you what His voice sounds like, safety feels like, and righteous authority looks like. As He does, what was once a wound becomes wisdom and what was meant to destroy your faith becomes the very place where it is made stronger.

Chapter 2
Authority Belongs to Christ Alone
Red Flag: **Centralized Authority**

"And when they had ordained them elders in every church, and had prayed with fasting, they commended them to the Lord..." **(Acts 14:23 KJV)**. The Body of Christ was never designed to be a one-man empire. Yet across America today with increasing regularity, we see ministries where all authority, decision making, and spiritual power is centralized in one individual. It's presented as strength, prophetic authority, and apostolic leadership. However, according to Scripture it's everything God warned us against. The early church was not built around one superstar preacher with a staff of silent *"yes men"*. It was built around plurality and a shared leadership model saturated in prayer, humility, and mutual accountability. In every city, there were elders, not one elder. There were shepherds, not a lone shepherd. God distributed authority on purpose to protect His people and glorify His Son.

The Church Is a Body, not a Hierarchy
Paul describes the church as diverse, dependent, and whole. No single part, not even the head, can claim supremacy because *"...Christ is the head of the church..."* **(Ephesians 5:23 ESV)**.
Yet in certain ministries the pastor becomes the:
- head in practice
- final word
- unquestionable authority
- source of vision, power, and even identity for the congregation

Instead of Christ at the center, it is the man on the platform. When that happens, the church stops functioning like a body and starts resembling a business with the pastor as *CEO* and everyone else as disposable employees or clients. Jesus said, *"...But it shall not be so among you..."* **(Mark 10:42-43 ESV)**. Greatness in the kingdom is not measured by how many obey you but by how many you serve.

Authority Goes Too Far

The Old Testament gives us a stark example in King Uzziah. He was blessed, strong, and favored by God until he let power deceive him: *"But when he was strong, his heart was lifted up to his destruction..."* **(2 Chronicles 26:16 KJV)**. King Uzziah decided that because he was king, he could also be priest. He crossed the line; God judged him instantly. Why? Because God never gave one man all roles.

The Scripture gives us another glimpse in a lesser-known leader, Diotrephes, *"...who loveth to have the pre-eminence among them..."* **(3 John 1:9 KJV)**. He wanted to be first, honored, and have control. He rejected apostolic authority, spoke malicious words against others, and even expelled church members who disagreed. John the Apostle did not soften it or excuse it. He exposed it as sin. A leader who controls is not a leader in the Spirit of Christ.

Even Peter Was Corrected

No one was more visible in the early church than Peter. He walked on water, saw Jesus transfigured, and preached at Pentecost. Yet when he was in error, Paul confronted him publicly: *"...I withstood him to the face..."* **(Galatians 2:11 KJV)**. The model of leadership in

God's house is not one man elevated above everyone else; it is one body submitted to one Head, Jesus Christ.

Only One Voice Matters

Things we have seen in Scripture such as shared authority, mutual correction, and servants instead of lords was the exact opposite of what I came to experience in this ministry. When I first joined, I believed with all my heart that I was stepping into a place where truth and boldness reigned. The sermons were fiery, worship was passionate, crowds were growing, and the voice of the wolf felt like the voice of conviction. Over time the voice of Christ was replaced by the voice of one man. Questions were not just ignored, they were forbidden. Concerns were not discussed, they were silenced. Decisions were not shared, they were dictated. It took me years of watching, serving, and enduring to finally recognize what the Scriptures had been warning me about all along. When you centralize authority in one person, you're no longer building the Body of Christ, you're building a kingdom of men; it will always, always, come crumbling down.

As our time in ministry continued, the reality of what was happening beneath the surface began to unfold before me. What once felt like bold Spirit led leadership, revealed itself to be something else entirely, a tightly controlled environment where all authority, especially financial and spiritual authority, was centralized in two people, the wolf and false prophetess. They were the sole decision makers, gatekeepers, and unquestioned heads of all operations. No one, not even ordained pastors had any real access to the decisions they were making. Nothing was transparent. There was no financial board, eldership, or team of accountable leaders. It was just the two of them. No one else was permitted to see the books. Everything from tithes and offerings to major purchases was controlled solely by them behind closed doors, which is not only unwise but unbiblical: *"Providing for honest things, not only in the sight of the Lord, but also in the sight of men"* **(2 Corinthians 8:21 KJV).**

Biblical stewardship isn't just about being faithful before God, it's about being honest with people too. That is why churches appoint multiple elders, deacons, and overseers, so that no one person will fall into the snare of self-serving authority or unchecked power. Yet the exact opposite was happening here.

In 2024, the church raised nearly $2 million for a future building, a vision we all believed in, sacrificed for, and stood behind with faith. After the deal fell through, the money did not re-enter a communal or accountable space. Instead, we were soon told that the wolf and false prophetess were purchasing a $1.6 million home, which we later found out was under the church's name. Shortly afterwards the wolf's wife made a comment to me and my wife. She stated throughout their whole ministry they had always put the church first, but this time they were going to put themselves first. Little did I know, she was referring to a luxury home which had been renovated, upgraded, and decorated with the best of the best. This also included the purchase of a $40,000 camper for their ex-son-in-law to live in. This was taking place while some church members were struggling to keep their lights on in their own homes. Meanwhile, the wolf would ask his congregation to *"give until it hurts"* or *"If you are faithful with God's money, He will bless you"* during the weekly tithe campaign. When the church purchase deal fell through, all of us were being shamed to believe that we were the reason that we didn't get the new church. The staff members of the church were told nothing until the purchase of the home was complete. There was no vote, discussion, or accountability, just a mention of *"God's blessing"* from the pulpit. God's Word does not support backroom blessings: *"...in the multitude of counsellors there is safety"* **(Proverbs 11:14 KJV)**.

The spending didn't start with the 1.6-million-dollar home. In 2021, they bought a modular home and acreage on the previous church property and remodeled it with extravagant features including a hot tub, sauna, pool, additional living space, greenhouse that was never used, garage for the wolf's multiple bikes, and another small home built behind their home for their son, all funded and furnished under the church's name. When it was done, it was not used for ministry. It was remodeled from top to bottom at the church's expense and used for themselves. I understand that the wolf and false prophetess needed a place to live. This isn't the issue; the issue lies with the fact that there was no approval or accountability for expenses. There was unlimited funding; they decided how much would be spent on themselves.

Later, we came to understand that another modular home and acreage had also been purchased in the church's name, was remodeled and given to their daughter without any church approval or oversight. Meanwhile, staff pastors couldn't get clarity on budgets for benevolence or needs within the church. At this time, we offered our congregants nothing in addition to Sunday and Wednesday services. The financial favor always seemed to flow upward, before it flowed outward, first to the leadership's benefit, then if there was anything left over, it went to the congregation's needs. Jesus spoke directly to this kind of behavior when He confronted the Pharisees: *"But he that is greatest among you shall be your servant"* **(Matthew 23:11 KJV)**.

What we were witnessing was not servanthood, it was entitlement. While individuals and families in the church privately reached out for support, the wolf and false prophetess were remodeling their home, installing pools and privacy fences, purchasing new vehicles, and requiring silence as the price for staying in their pack. That silence extended well beyond money.

As staff pastors, we were publicly positioned as leaders yet privately denied the ability to lead. The wolf's wife controlled every facet of ministry with an iron grip. We could not make decisions without her approval. We could not change anything in our areas of care, counseling, ministry flow, or event size. Sermons were no longer allowed to be led by the Holy Spirit, but we were asked to preach about *"house values"*. The false prophetess even requested our staff pastors' sermon notes for approval. Kasey and I were strong in this area; we never once submitted our sermon notes or preached a house value. We didn't even preach an online Bible study for the last year of our employment, but we paid the price for it. Worship songs couldn't be written without her approval; every aspect of the ministry was controlled by her, even down to what color the walls should be painted in the sanctuary. We were the face; she was the force. If what we felt led did not align with her preferences, we were accused of not being *"submitted to the house."* We did not *"hear from God"* and we were *"in rebellion."* Repeatedly she weaponized spirituality to maintain control stating, *"I'm always in the throne room of Heaven."* The false prophetess was basically saying if we were not aligned with her vision, then we were not aligned with God. We were told that questioning decisions was equivalent to questioning what the Lord had directed her to do. That's not submission; that is spiritual manipulation: *"Woe be unto the pastors that destroy and scatter the*

43

sheep of my pasture! saith the Lord" **(Jeremiah 23:1 KJV)**.
You cannot claim to shepherd God's people while
silencing their God given discernment. Make no
mistake, spiritual censorship was part of the culture.
There was no hiring process or leadership development.
People would show up on staff with no conversation or
clarity, just *"meet your new coworker."* By the end of
2025, staff members still lacked clarity about their roles
and responsibilities, while decision-making remained
solely in the hands of the wolf and the false prophetess.
Staff members were removed suddenly and silently.
One day they were there and the next day they were
gone. We were given generic answers as to why they
were let go and never had the ability to question it. We
were never allowed to speak of it again.
I spoke to a staff member who worked with us from
2022-2025 and was recently let go. She was told one
reason in a meeting with the wolf as to why she got
fired but never given the opportunity to prove the
accusations that had been brought against her were
untrue, even though she had documented proof. She and
her husband later had a meeting with the wolf and his
wife. In this meeting, the wolf told her that she was
being let go to protect the relationship between her and
his wife, the false prophetess. When they stated that this
was not the reason that was given to her in the previous
meeting, the wolf acted confused and ultimately
dismissed them without clarification. No one on staff or
in the congregation knew why she was let go, left the
church, or stripped from her duties over a large group
of people. Even today, that staff member is still
questioning the real reason as to why she was
terminated. This is not how the Body of Christ operates.
This is how a spiritual dictatorship functions.
Ordination eventually became another form of control.
Six staff members were ordained as staff pastors in less

than a year, not based on calling but compliance. The wolf's wife, the false prophetess, chose those she knew would submit to her will. She ordained those she could spiritually manage, those that did not challenge her, were young, impressionable, eager to serve, and blind to the system they were walking into.

She said, *"God had called them."* However, two of them personally told me that they were not called to be staff pastors and did not want to be ordained. Nevertheless, they allowed themselves to be called a staff pastor. We must understand, what God calls, God qualifies, not manipulates. They were not being raised up to lead; they were being positioned to obey.

When a leader uses their influence to silence, exclude, belittle, and spiritually intimidate, it's not the Holy Spirit speaking; it's pride. Pride is the quickest way for ministries to fall. I wish I had known then what I know now. I would have pushed back and sounded the alarm, but the truth is, I did not. I was groomed to believe this was normal. I was afraid of being the problem, disloyal, losing my position, and worse, my sense of calling. Slowly, painfully, and undeniably, the Lord began to open my eyes. He reminded me: *"ye shall know the truth, and the truth shall make you free"* **(John 8:32 KJV)**, not loyalty, silence, or compliance but ***Truth***. I have surrendered to the Lord, even if it cost me everything.

Love Requires Leaving

There is a peculiar kind of ache that settles into your soul when truth makes you walk away from what once felt like home. It is not loud at first. It whispers through the cracks in your convictions in the praying hours of the night and shows up in tears spilled on pages of Scripture, especially the ones that no longer align with the life you're living, the leadership you're serving under, and the gospel you're preaching through compromised lips. Through the ache of awakening my wife and I began to realize the gentleness of the Lord. He persistently and undeniably started revealing the difference between the church we were in and the church He had designed. The church we were in revolved around the approval of the wolf and the false prophetess. They operated their church under the illusion of unity built on fear, silence, and unquestioned loyalty. The Bible we read explains the church revolves around the Father, Son, and the Holy Spirit, three as One (the Trinity). Scripture also explains that unity is built on the Holy Spirit speaking truth in love, not suppression or buried under spiritual intimidation: *"But speaking the truth in love, may grow up into him in all things, which is the head, even Christ"* **(Ephesians 4:15 KJV)**. It was in the quiet corners of Scripture that the stories of Paul confronting Peter, Nathan rebuking David, and God calling His leaders back to humility, that we realized what God was trying to show us. This is not a path of rebellion or betrayal but a path of returning.

Returning to God's Blueprint

Slowly, the Lord began to rebuild our understanding of how He intended the Church to function as a living, breathing, and Christ centered Body, where every member matters, every gift has value, every leader is accountable, and no human voice has the right to silence the Spirit of God in another. There should not be a wolf circus or false prophetess. Father reminded us of the way the early church operated as a family marked by plurality in leadership, mutual submission, and radical transparency, not as a hierarchical company with one human CEO. That is why:

- they had elders, not an emperor

46

- they conducted public accountability, not hidden accusations
- no one person had preeminence because Jesus alone had that place

"For other foundation can no man lay than that is laid, which is Jesus Christ" **(1 Corinthians 3:11 KJV)**. We had learned dependency on leadership, seen praise given to personality, and lived in fear of questioning. The Word taught us to depend on Christ and give Him all glory and Honor. The Word instructs us to: *"...try the spirits whether they are of God: because many false prophets are gone out into the world"* **(1 John 4:1 KJV)**. The Spirit of the Lord was instructing us to use discernment because we are going to be faced with many deceptions in the last days. He invited us back to the heart of His Church which is led by shepherds founded on truth and flourishing in accountability. He does not need wolves, hirelings, Ahabs or Jezebels but men and women to stand for the truth at the ultimate show down. When we tested the spirits by the Word it was obvious that we were being deceived in plain sight. The truth would not allow us to continue to work in this manipulation (which is a form of witchcraft). We could not keep calling something *"church"* when it looked more like a brand, business, or at worst a trap or even a cult. *"Now the Lord is that Spirit: and where the Spirit of the Lord is, there is liberty"* **(2 Corinthians 3:17 KJV)**. Once freedom found us, we knew it was now our responsibility to walk in it.

The Breaking Point of Love

There came a moment, a quiet but seismic moment, when loyalty to Jesus meant disloyalty to what was being done in His name. That moment was not easy; it meant letting go of what we had built, celebrated, and called to do. This meant we had to face accusations of rebellion, betrayal, and disobedience, not just from leadership but from people we loved, served, and pastored.

You must understand the culture enforced when someone left the church or no longer worked there. People were often ostracized, unfriended, and treated as if they were never a part of the Body of Christ. They were plagued because they decided to walk away from this particular church. The reason congregants would act this way is because it was preached from the pulpit. If this is happening within your church, let it be a red flag warning to you that they are not operating as the true Body of Christ but as a spiritual dictatorship. People are allowed to leave churches and to have a difference in opinion. It doesn't make them evil, witches, or spiritually incorrect. Even Jesus allowed people to leave without trying to destroy their character. We were never called to stop loving people because they decided to leave a church.

After seeing all these things, it was in that moment of clarity that Father whispered something into our spirits that only sounded like peace: *"You do not stay silent to protect their church. You speak truth to protect My people."* That's when we knew. Leaving was not an act of bitterness; it was an act of obedience. It was not running from conflict but running toward Christ. The deeper we ran toward Him, the clearer it all became; this is not what Jesus died to build. The church is not meant to be a house of silent servants cowering under manmade authority; it is meant to be a place where every believer, voice, and gift can express the fullness of Christ in the safety of love, truth, and accountability. Freedom is not loud or vengeful. It is quiet, powerful, and courageous to walk in truth, even if it costs you everything that is not built on Him. Everything else is sinking sand.

Healing from One-Person Authority

When authority is revolved around one person, the church quietly shifts from being the Body of Christ to orbiting around a single voice. What may begin as a vision or strong leadership can slowly harden into control. Scripture never compromises, **Christ alone is the head of the Church**: *"And he is the head of the body, the church..."* **(Colossians 1:18 KJV)**. When that truth is eclipsed by personality, platform, or power, spiritual imbalance follows.

Many who come out of a leader-controlled system feel disoriented because they were trained to look to one person other than Christ for direction, affirmation, and spiritual covering. Over time, discernment is outsourced, conscience suppressed, and Scripture filtered through a single interpretive lens. The Word never presents authority as singular and unchecked. Instead, it describes a plurality of elders, mutual submission, and shared discernment: *"And he gave some, apostles; and some, prophets; and some, evangelists; and some, pastors and teachers"* **(Ephesians 4:11 KJV)**. Authority in the church was designed to be distributed, not monopolized.

Healing begins when believers relearn that submission to Christ does not require surrendering their God given discernment to one leader. The Holy Spirit was not given to one man for the sake of all; He was poured out on all flesh **(Acts 2:17 KJV)**. Every believer is indwelt, guided, and taught by God **(John 14:26 KJV)**. When authority revolves around one person, people are subtly taught to distrust the Spirit in themselves while elevating the Spirit in the leader. Healing reverses that distortion by restoring confidence in the Holy Spirit's work within the whole body.

One of the most damaging effects of a one-person authority is fear of being *"out from under covering,"* missing God, and punishment for leaving. Yet Scripture teaches that believers are already secure in Christ: *"And ye are complete in him…"* **(Colossians 2:10 KJV)**. No man stands between you and God as a necessary mediator: *"For there is one God, and one mediator between God and men, the man Christ Jesus"* **(1 Timothy 2:5 KJV)**. Healing comes when people realize they did not lose God by leaving a system; they removed themselves from a structure God never designed. Rebuilding a healthy leadership requires true repentance. Jesus walked in true humility, while others should be serving Him, He was serving them. Does your leader serve like Jesus demonstrated?

Scripture repeatedly warns against elevating one person above the body. Paul confronted the Corinthian church for dividing themselves around individual leaders: *"…I am of Paul; and another, I am of Apollos…"* **(1 Corinthians 3:4 KJV)**. His response was clear; no mortal person is the foundation: *"For other foundation can no man lay than that is laid, which is Jesus Christ"* **(1 Corinthians 3:11 KJV)**. Healing includes repenting of leader dependence and re-anchoring faith in Christ alone. Healthy churches cultivate shared leadership, transparency, and accountability. Even apostles submitted to one another and to the counsel of the church **(Acts 15:6; Galatians 2:9 KJV)**. Authority that cannot be questioned is not biblical authority; it is power unchecked. Healing often means learning to trust environments where leaders invite accountability rather than resist it and unity is built on truth rather than control.

For many, healing also requires forgiving the self-centered leader or leaders' authority. They are by no means excused from their misguidance, but the effected congregants need to release the hold it has on their heart. The only way is *forgiveness*, so it does not lead to *bitterness*. Forgiveness breaks the cycle of fear and bitterness, allowing God to restore peace (*Ephesians 4:31–32* KJV). As trust is rebuilt, believers rediscover that Christ governs His Church faithfully without human coercion (the act of forcing, pressuring, or intimidating someone to do something against their will, usually through threats, manipulation, fear, or abusive power): *"...the government shall be upon his shoulder..."* (*Isaiah 9:6* KJV). He does not abdicate His throne to any man. Ultimately, healing from authority revolving around one person leads believers back to a living, breathing dependence on Christ as Head. It restores the beauty of the body functioning together, each part supplying what the other lacks (*1 Corinthians 12:14–27* KJV). What once felt fragile becomes strong again, not because power is reclaimed but because it is properly placed. When authority returns to Christ, the church becomes what it was always meant to be, a people led by the Holy Spirit (Ruach HaKodesh), grounded in truth and free from fear.

51

Chapter 3
Leaders Elevated Above the Flock

One of the most troubling patterns in abusive or unhealthy church systems is the elevation of leaders as spiritually superior to the rest of the congregation. It's not always said out loud. Sometimes, it's subtle, just a tone, language, or an assumed authority. Over time you start to notice only certain people are seen as truly *"spiritual,"* while everyone else is expected to follow and fall in line. That is not how the church was designed to operate.

The Bible teaches that we are all one body, equally loved by God, indwelt by the Spirit, able to hear from Him, and walk in His power. When leaders elevate themselves above other believers spiritually, they're not just misusing authority, they're actively denying the identity of the people of God as a kingdom of priests: *"But ye are a chosen generation, a royal priesthood, a holy nation, a peculiar people..."* **(1 Peter 2:9 KJV)**. *You* are part of God's holy priesthood, not just the pastor, prophet, or *"anointed"* inner circle staff.

When a leader tells you that you're not hearing from God clearly or that only they can discern God's voice on a higher level, they're undermining what Jesus died to give you, access to the Father.

Leaders Exalting Themselves Spiritually
When pastors or leaders spiritually elevate themselves, it creates a culture where people become silent.

Spiritual insecurity takes root. You start doubting your own ability to hear or discern truth. You hesitate to speak and rely on someone else for decisions only you and God were ever meant to make: *"For God hath not given us the spirit of fear..."* (**2 Timothy 1:7** KJV). Fear is not from the Father.

The moment only one person's spiritual voice matters, the rest of the body becomes stifled. The gifts stop flowing, worship becomes controlled, and ministry becomes manufactured. The freedom of the Holy Spirit is replaced by the comfort of control: *"Now the Lord is that Spirit: and where the Spirit of the Lord is, there is liberty"* (**2 Corinthians 3:17** KJV). Liberty goes missing under spiritual superiority. When the Holy Spirit is absent, so is true freedom.

When people are told they need a leader to *"hear from God for them,"* they stop growing, reading the Word for themselves, or allowing the Spirit to instruct and convict personally. Eventually, they are spiritually dependent on the leader rather than dependent on the Lord. This is not discipleship. It's spiritual enslavement.

Recognizing a Red Flag in Your Church

Here are some signs indicating that your pastor or leadership may have elevated themselves spiritually above others:

- They constantly imply they have unique spiritual access others do not.
- You are discouraged or even shamed for hearing differently than they claim to.
- They use *"God told me"* as a way to end conversations rather than open them.
- They tell you to trust their discernment more than your own.
- They imply you're spiritually immature if you question anything they say.

- The congregation's identity is built around the pastor's voice, not Christ's.
- Those closest to leadership are treated as more spiritually favored.

Ask yourself, do I feel empowered in my walk with Jesus or dependent on someone else to walk it for me? If the answer is the latter, then you are not in a discipleship environment, you are in a controlled system. The truth is simple and worth stating clearly; leadership does not make someone more spiritual, loudness does not make someone more anointed, and a title does not make someone closer to God. Jesus made every believer worthy of the Father's presence: *"...we have boldness and access with confidence by the faith of him"* **(Ephesians 3:12 KJV)**. You don't need a pastor, prophet, or *"apostolic covering"* to enter God's presence. You need Jesus and you already have Him. One of the most painful and dangerous patterns I witnessed in this ministry was the elevation of leadership to near divine status. It was not spoken from the pulpit in so many words, but it was communicated in everything they did. They were not just pastors. They were *"God's chosen voice."* They were the appointed *"gatekeepers of revelation."* Their spiritual authority was not something they stewarded; it was something they weaponized. What started as respect for leadership slowly morphed into an unspoken belief that the pastors were closer to God than the rest of us. Their opinions carried the weight of Scripture, preferences became church doctrine, visions were labeled as God's direction, and their choices were not to be questioned. To question them was to question God Himself. The false prophetess would say things like, *"I have been in the throne room with the Lord. If you disagree with me, you're disagreeing with the Voice of God in my life."* To the outside world, it might sound bold, spiritual, or even prophetic, but inside the hearts of those under that leadership, spiritual inferiority took root. People stopped trusting their own ability to hear from God. They began to second guess their discernment. Their intimacy with Jesus became dependent upon another's approval. The lie settled in: *"I need them to be close to God, because I am not enough."* That is not the gospel of Jesus Christ: *"For there is one God, and one mediator between God and men, the man Christ Jesus"* (**1 Timothy 2:5 KJV**).

There is no spiritual ladder in the Kingdom of God. There is no preferential access to His presence for those with microphones, titles, or platforms. Every believer has the right and the invitation to come boldly into the presence of God (**Hebrews 4:16 KJV**). When a leader positions themself as the exclusive voice for God, they move from shepherd to spiritual tyrant. The damage is deep. People in such environments often feel spiritually stunted, emotionally exhausted, and unworthy of hearing from God outside the filter of a human mediator. Slowly, a dangerous dependence is formed, not on Christ but on the leader. That is not discipleship, that's bondage.

Spiritual superiority is subtle but devastating. A pastor who believes they hear from God more than everyone else will always surround themselves with people who follow without question. They will ordain those who don't challenge them. They will create inner circles based on loyalty, not calling. The body becomes fractured, leaders at the top, servants at the bottom, and voices of truth drowned out by applause. Jesus never endorsed spiritual elitism. In fact, He condemned it: *"But be not ye called Rabbi: for one is your Master, even Christ; and all ye are brethren"* (**Matthew 23:8 KJV**). All are brethren, equal, and partners in grace and truth.

Christ alone is the Master, everyone else is a servant. Yet in this ministry, titles did not serve people. People served titles. We were told that the pastors had *"levels of spiritual access"* we were still *"growing into."* That they had a deeper connection to the voice of God. If we heard something different, something that did not align with their preferences, the assumption was that we were immature, deceived, or rebellious. The Bible says the opposite: *"My sheep hear my voice, and I know them, and they follow me"* **(John 10:27 KJV)**. Jesus did not say, *"My sheep hear their pastor's voice."* He said they hear *His voice*. That means every believer, no matter their title, has access to the Shepherd's heart. When leaders elevate themselves above the flock, they distort the gospel and suppress the Holy Spirit's work in others. People walk in fear of being *"out of alignment."* They crave approval instead of intimacy and let others define their calling because they no longer trust their own connection to Christ. That's not leadership, that's control. It's not shepherding but spiritual suffocation. True biblical leadership does not put itself on a pedestal. It gets on its knees. True shepherds don't build platforms, they build people. They don't demand honor; they earn it by serving. Jesus showed us the way: *"Even as the Son of man came not to be ministered unto, but to minister, and to give his life a ransom for many"* **(Matthew 20:28 KJV)**.

If leaders are unwilling to serve with transparency, to be held accountable, or to honor the spiritual voice of every member of the body, they are not following Jesus. They are performing a role He never assigned. The church deserves better because the Spirit of God is not poured out on the elite; *it is poured out on all flesh* **(Joel 2:28 KJV)**. Men, women, young, old, pastors, congregants, teachers, and children all can have access to the Father's heart. We don't need a person to stand in the way of that. Instead, we all need Jesus and Jesus alone.

As the Lord revealed the truth about spiritual humility and servant leadership through His Word, I could not deny one heartbreaking reality. Everything I was seeing in Scripture was at odds with what I was living in the ministry I served. The *red flag* of spiritual superiority was not just theoretical; it was woven into the fabric of our church culture. I was not just hearing about it; I was under it. I watched sincere believers doubt their walk with God because they did not have the wolf's *"level of access."* I saw people deceived because their discernment did not align with the false prophetess' *"fresh word from the throne room."* I personally lived through moments where the leadership's elevated status was used not to shepherd the flock but to suppress, intimidate, and emotionally control those of us called to serve. What I experienced was not spiritual leadership; it was spiritual manipulation. Oh boy, did it ever come at a great cost!

Now, I want to share with you what I lived on the inside. What happens when leaders place themselves above the body and what does that do to the heart of a servant trying to obey God during it all? Let me take you to the place I once was and never want to return to again. In our church, honor was not something we lived; it was something we demanded. So much so that *"honor"* became one of our official house values, not as an expression of Christ like humility but as a constant reminder for the people to reverence the pastors. Titles were everything. Every staff member who was ordained had to be addressed as *"Pastor"* not as Justin or Kasey. Pastors did not have personalities; they had pedestals. It was our job to make sure everyone kept it that way.

We were explicitly instructed if we ever heard someone address a pastor by their first name alone, we were required to stop them immediately, correct and rebuke them. If they did it again, they were not just being casual; they were dishonorable. That word *"dishonorable"* was used like a gavel, slamming down on anyone who refused to bow to the culture of reverence that we were told to uphold. The false prophetess went live on Facebook regarding this topic and it's still on the Internet today. She told us, *"When I hear someone refer to a pastor by their first name, it makes me want to scratch their eyeballs out."* In this context, she was referring to staff and congregants alike. Honor was not something that flowed but a weapon. The dividing line was crystal clear. We did not just have a staff but a staff class with a chosen few in a tight circle. It was an untouchable group. Congregants could serve, give, and attend but they could not belong unless they played by the unspoken rules, worshipped the personalities, and never asked to be treated as equals. Kasey and I were known among the staff as *"the people pastors."* We were the ones who often took the phone calls, sat with the hurting, held the hands, and prayed the late-night prayers. I am by no means saying that other staff pastors and staff members didn't do this as well, but they recognized our loyalty to serving the people.

In 2023, we were burning ourselves out trying to serve people and being the best little *"pastor slaves"* as possible, serving the people God sent to us. The wolf, false prophetess, and select staff members were holding private parties on the church property but not for the congregants. Kasey and I were not invited and they did not try to hide it. They would host these parties during Saturday night prayer meetings. Yes, while people cried out for God in the sanctuary and deliverances happened at the altar with tears and spiritual warfare, we literally heard the staff laughing, splashing in the pool, playing music, and enjoying themselves just outside the sanctuary walls. They did not bother to be discreet. The message felt loud and clear, *"This is us. That is, **you**. Don't get confused."* We weren't just excluded, we were made to hear the separation. It was not just Kasey and I, but congregants also saw it. They could hear the music and the laughter coming from the wolf's home while the people worshipped alone in the next building. Some even approached us asking, *"Why are they partying instead of praying?"* None of us had an answer that did not break our hearts.

This culture of exclusion did not end at pool parties. Selective invitation was a way of life. There were birthday celebrations, private meals, and catered events including a birthday party for the wolf's daughter which was held directly after a Sunday morning service in which the in-house security was assigned to block the doors. A high-end hibachi chef had been hired to cook a private dinner and only those on the list were allowed inside. Shockingly, only 4 staff members weren't invited, Kasey and I included in that number. Even congregants who gave sacrificially and tithed, prayed, and served were not allowed to attend.

Honor, in our house, was not mutual; it was manipulation. From the pulpit, the false prophetess would repeatedly say *"Y'all just don't get it, do you?"* No, we did not *"get it."* What she called *"authority"* was really spiritual elitism and what she called *"access"* was actual segregation. Her perspective of *"God's order"* was nothing more than a system designed to keep some people *"in"* and everyone else *"out."* In other words, you were either in the click or out of the click. We watched the emotional cost of it all unfold. People whose hearts were open, hungry, and seeking God, were made to feel small, unworthy, and not spiritual enough.

In 2022-2023, our church began leaning more into deliverance ministry. The leadership created a *"deliverance team,"* a group of specially chosen individuals who were permitted to cast out demons, counsel the afflicted, and pray with authority; not just anyone could be part of it. This team was handpicked by the wolf, false prophetess and deliverance leader. Even devoted, Spirit filled church members who completed the mandatory training and passed the written test were not guaranteed a place on the team. Their eligibility did not depend on their maturity, fruit, or calling. It depended solely on the leader's personal judgment of their *"spiritual character."* Time and time again, I watched faithful believers, people who had served, prayed, tithed, and loved deeply, take the course, pass the test, and still be told they were not permitted to operate in deliverance. Not only that, but they were not even allowed to pray over others within the church setting. The message was clear, only a hand selected few were safe. Only certain people had *"enough discernment."* Others were treated as potential witches or warlocks. It did not matter how long they had been in the church or how much fruit was in their life. Suspicion overruled the Holy Spirit. Though the strict *"deliverance only"* team is not what's present in the church today, the pattern has not changed, it's only shifted. The same exclusivity and spiritual manipulation now exist in the form of a segregated prayer team created in 2025. Only those chosen by leadership are allowed to *"carry"* the weight of intercession. Only those approved are considered *"safe"* enough to pray for specific needs of the church. Those members aren't safe either though, if they missed prayer times due to their schedule, they would be removed because they weren't dedicated enough. What began as deliverance ended in division and it taught people to fear one another more than to rely on the Holy Spirit.

As time went on, things seemed to get worse when theology was skewed to protect the pedestal. I once sat in the hospitality room with the false prophetess. She explained that she was *"covered,"* and could no longer sin. She declared, *"I don't even think I'm capable of sin anymore."* Yet moments later, she preached about repentance to the congregation, contradicting herself without a trace of self-awareness or humility.

This is what spiritual superiority looks like in real time, abuse of authority masked as anointing, isolation parading as holiness, and favoritism passing itself off as discernment. We lived it, day after day. At first, we were deceived in believing this behavior was normal. Then we realized what it was doing to us and other people. The Lord whispered, *"This is not My Kingdom. This is theirs."*

Through everything I have walked through in this ministry, God has been faithful to not only expose what was unhealthy but also to remind me of what is true. He did not leave me in confusion or bitterness. Instead, He led me back to the heart of His Church which is built on Christ, love, and truth. It does not consist of control, manipulation, or fear. God showed me that honor was never meant to be demanded, controlled, or enforced. True honor flows naturally from a heart transformed by Christ. When it is weaponized, it ceases to be honor at all. That kind of *"honor"* turns people into tools of someone else's vision rather than sons and daughters of God. The Lord reminded me that the church was never meant to elevate one personality as the image of God. There is only one foundation for the Church, and His name is Jesus Christ **(1 Corinthians 3:11 KJV)**.

He also showed me something deeply personal, I was not wrong for questioning what I saw. I was not rebellious for feeling unsettled or dishonorable for being grieved in my spirit. I was discerning and that mattered to God. I had been taught that loyalty meant silence, but God taught me that loyalty to Him sometimes means being a voice that will speak when no one else will. I had confused charisma for calling, mistaken control for order, and allowed what was familiar to blind me to what was unbiblical. Through His Word, God reminded me of what His Church was always meant to look like, a place where the Holy Spirit leads, humility reigns, and every believer has access to His presence, not just a select few. He showed me that the Kingdom of God is not built on platforms but on people. It does not need spiritual elites or more control. It needs spiritual servants and freedom. I now understand that God's Church does not belong to any pastor, movement, or personality. It belongs to Him. We don't get to gatekeep His presence or pick who is worthy of His Spirit. We absolutely do not have the right to silence or shame those He calls. God used this experience to purify my own heart. He reminded me that I am His son, not someone's pawn. I am called to walk in truth and help protect the people of God from deception. If telling this story helps even one person find the courage to ask hard questions, press back against manipulation, or trust Jesus again, then everything I have been through will have been worth it. He has not called me to tear down the church but help set captives free. He is rebuilding His Church, not on spiritual intimidation but on the blood of His Son, the leadership of His Spirit, and the truth of His Word. A wise man once said, *"You can overlook their past, but you can't overlook their patterns."* I agree, past can be overlooked, but patterns are intentional and what is done in the darkness, always comes to light.

Leaders Rise Above the Flock

There is a subtle shift that happens when leaders stop seeing themselves as servants of the flock and begin to see themselves as separate from it. It does not always begin loudly. It often begins with language, *"God speaks to me differently," "I'm held to a higher standard," "You would not understand at your level."* Over time, distinction becomes distance, distance becomes manipulation, and manipulation becomes spiritual superiority. What was meant to be shepherding quietly turns into elevation. Scripture confronts this directly. Peter exhorts leaders to *"Feed the flock of God... neither as being lords over God's heritage, but being examples to the flock"* **(1 Peter 5:2–3 KJV)**. The moment a leader places themselves above correction, accountability, or the very people they are called to serve, they are no longer functioning as a shepherd; they are ruling as a lord. Christ explicitly forbade this posture among His followers. Jesus warned that religious leaders who exalt themselves spiritually would eventually devour the very people they claim to lead: *"They love the uppermost rooms at feasts, and the chief seats in the synagogues... and to be called of men, Rabbi, Rabbi"* **(Matthew 23:6–7 KJV)**. He went on to say, *"But he that is greatest among you shall be your servant. And whosoever shall exalt himself shall be abased..."* **(Matthew 23:11–12 KJV)**. Spiritual superiority is not a mark of holiness; it is a warning sign of pride. When leaders elevate themselves above the flock, they often spiritualize their authority to silence dissent. Questioning becomes rebellion, discernment becomes dishonor, and disagreement becomes evidence of immaturity. This posture trains believers to distrust their own conscience and exalt the leader's voice above Scripture. Yet the Bible declares, *"But ye have an unction from the Holy One, and ye know all things"* (**1 John 2:20** KJV). God did not give discernment to a select few. He gave His Spirit to His people.

The damage caused by spiritual superiority is profound. It fractures identity because believers begin to measure their worth by proximity to power rather than proximity to Christ. It breeds fear because leaders who believe they are spiritually superior often believe they are spiritually untouchable. It distorts the image of God, presenting Him as distant, hierarchical, and inaccessible. Scripture reveals Him as near, humble, and gentle: *"The LORD is nigh unto all them that call upon him..."* (**Psalm 145:18** KJV).

Healing begins when the lie is exposed. No leader stands above the flock as a spiritual elite: *"For all have sinned, and come short of the glory of God"* (**Romans 3:23** KJV). Titles do not sanctify character; platforms do not exempt anyone from accountability. Even apostles referred to themselves as fellow servants, not spiritual aristocracy. Paul called himself *"...less than the least of all saints..."* (**Ephesians 3:8** KJV), not because he lacked authority but because he understood it correctly. One of the greatest acts of healing is reclaiming your equal standing before God. Scripture declares that believers are *"...a chosen generation, a royal priesthood..."* (**1 Peter 2:9** KJV), not a priesthood led by a spiritual elite but a people made holy together. Access to God was purchased by Christ's blood, not granted by human permission: *"Having therefore, brethren, boldness to enter into the holiest by the blood of Jesus"* (**Hebrews 10:19** KJV). Jesus Himself dismantled spiritual superiority by the way He led. Though He was Lord of all, He knelt and washed feet (*John 13:3–5* KJV). He did not distance Himself from weakness; He drew near to it:

"Take my yoke upon you… for I am meek and lowly in heart…" **(Matthew 11:29 KJV)**. Any leadership that contradicts the posture of Christ is misrepresenting Jesus.

Healing also requires releasing the false belief that you are inferior for questioning, leaving, or seeing clearly. Scripture never condemns sheep for recognizing danger. Jesus said, *"When ye therefore shall see the abomination… Then let them which be in Judaea flee…"* **(Matthew 24:15–16 KJV)**. Discernment that leads to departure is not betrayal; it is wisdom. God does not shame His people for protecting their souls. As healing progresses, the Holy Spirit restores spiritual confidence. Where intimidation once ruled, peace returns. Where voices were elevated above Scripture, the Word becomes alive again. Where leaders demanded reverence, Christ reclaims it: *"Neither be ye called masters: for one is your Master, even Christ"* **(Matthew 23:10 KJV)**. The soul begins to breathe again when authority is returned to its rightful place.

The final stage of healing is learning to recognize healthy leadership without idolizing it. God still calls shepherds, teachers, and pastors but never as replacements for Himself. Healthy leaders equip rather than exalt, serve rather than separate, and walk among the flock rather than above it: *"…be clothed with humility…"* **(1 Peter 5:5 KJV)** is not optional, it is the uniform of Godly authority. When spiritual superiority is dismantled, the church becomes safe again. The flock is nurtured. The believer who once felt small, silenced, or spiritually inferior stands restored. Understand this unshakable truth, you were never beneath the flock, you were part of it, and Christ Himself is your Shepherd.

Chapter 4
Blessing vs. Loyalty

Just as believers are warned not to enter into relationships lightly or without discernment, the same spiritual principle applies to ministries, perhaps even more urgently. When churches or spiritual leaders yoke themselves together for reasons other than shared conviction, calling, and truth they open the doors to manipulation, compromise, and eventually destruction. Whether the bond is created through financial incentives, mutual platform building, or backroom agreements that look holy onstage but hide worldly ambitions behind the curtain, God calls it what it is, ***disobedience***. The Bible is not silent about this behavior.

Unequal Yokes Lead to Corruption
"Be ye not unequally yoked together with unbelievers: for what fellowship hath righteousness with unrighteousness?..." **(2 Corinthians 6:14 KJV).** We often think this verse is only about marriage but it applies to every kind of partnership where hearts, values, and purpose are supposed to be united. When a ministry yokes itself to another church, pastor, or organization without testing the spirit and discerning the fruit, it invites rebellion into its house. A ministry built on the appearance of unity but founded on unequal foundations cannot stand in God's eyes very long. God did not call us to build large networks of wealthy pastors. He called us to build His Kingdom in purity. When the motives for connection are mixed with

influence, money, fame, and mutual defense, the yoke is unholy.

Financial Incentives as Bribes in Disguise

"A wicked man taketh a gift out of the bosom to pervert the ways of judgment" **(Proverbs 17:23 KJV)**. When pastors offer money, resources, or *"support"* in exchange for another pastor's loyalty, involvement, or public endorsement, it's not generosity but manipulation. It makes the Gospel transactional instead of transformational. It transforms fellowship into business deals and ministry into a marketing tool. Every time a leader says, *"We will help your ministry... if you will stay connected to us,"* they are no longer operating as shepherds, they have taken the role of spiritual salesmen. God calls it wicked. In the Kingdom, the only acceptable currency is love, truth, and obedience, not dollars, networks, and platforms.

Unity Without Truth Is Rebellion

"Can two walk together, except they be agreed?" **(Amos 3:3 KJV)**. Here's what this verse does not say, *"Can two walk together if they have the same logo, the same livestream vibe, and a shared enemy?"* No, agreement in Scripture is always founded on **truth**, not convenience. Two ministries may be in agreement about style, politics, or personality but if they are not united in righteousness, purity, and Biblical integrity, they are not *"walking together"* in the eyes of God. They're just walking in the same direction toward a cliff.

Financial Entanglements Corrupt Integrity

"Feed the flock of God... not for filthy lucre, but of a ready mind" **(1 Peter 5:2 KJV)**. When pastors use their

resources to buy connection, loyalty, or silence, the people of God suffer. The offering becomes polluted. Ministry becomes a ladder, not a calling. People are no longer seen as sheep but assets. This is why God's Word commands leaders to be free from the love of money and why Paul said he *"...coveted no man's silver, or gold, or apparel"* **(Acts 20:33 KJV)**. If ministry is funded by manipulation, it will bear the fruit of compromise. God showed me if a ministry has to pay other ministries to walk alongside it, even initially, then it is not walking with Jesus. In the ministry I served, I saw this red flag more than once. I watched the wolf build *"alliances"* through financial offerings and incentives. I watched other pastors gifted money, platform time, influence, or *"honor"* in exchange for participation, loyalty, or endorsement of our ministry. Over time, I started to see it clearly. These were not Kingdom connections. These were contracts disguised as covenant. It was not spiritual covering but spiritual credit. The cost both spiritually and emotionally was far deeper than I realized at the time. Let me take you into that story.

Purchased Partnerships

During my time in this ministry, I watched the wolf form many *"partnerships"* with other leaders, but most of them were not born from kingdom unity. They were built on financial exchange, unspoken obligation, and strategic alliance. One story stands out in particular. It happened when we first stepped into deliverance ministry. The wolf traveled to visit a high-profile deliverance minister, let's call him *Derek*. After the service, Derek invited the wolf back to the green room where they spoke for only a short time. Before leaving, the wolf pulled out his checkbook and wrote him a check for $20,000. Derek declined it at first.

He said he did not need the money but the wolf insisted. His exact words were: *"I'm sure there's something you could use it for. Aren't you in the process of buying a house?"* Derek stated that the down payment for the home was already covered, but the wolf pressed the issue until he accepted the check. Derek even warned him, *"This will not buy my friendship."* The wolf told him that was not the intention but over time it became clear that it was. During the next year, Derek became a main speaker at several of our church's biggest events. The wolf even featured him in a movie that his business produced, placing Derek's face on the front cover. They shared platforms, events, influence, and money. Eventually, something fell apart between them. The wolf returned to the pulpit and discredited Derek publicly with no warning, meeting, or private conversation. Derek later posted on Facebook that the public accusation was the first he had heard of the issue. There was no phone call or discussion, just public humiliation from someone who had once bought his *"friendship."* This was not the only *"so called"* kingdom partnership that turned transactional.

$700,000 Tent for Another Ministry

Another instance was especially shocking. The wolf and the false prophetess discovered another growing church led by leaders who called themselves *apostles*. They were expanding fast and needed a permanent structure for one of their locations. So, the wolf and false prophetess gave them $700,000, enough to build a permanent tent structure with automatic doors. Meanwhile, our own congregation was meeting in a broken-down location that was falling apart. The church family that had faithfully served, tithed, traveled, and sacrificed was left to gather in ruin, but a distant ministry was gifted nearly a million dollars to build what we could only dream of having. That $700,000 gift led to a tight alliance. Those *"apostles"* were brought into our inner circle and given platforms, praise, visibility, and substantial financial blessings every time they visited, even when they said they did not need a speaker fee. That relationship began to shape the culture of our own church. Soon, we were mirroring their model, introducing incentives that required people to pay money to attend, which we had never done before. Titles like *"apostle"* and *"prophet,"* were elevated and leaders were chosen on perceived loyalty instead of biblical calling.

The next red flag came through one of our *"house prophets,"* a man I once admired. During a service, he stood before the church and declared that the Lord had revealed a $100,000 financial need for the house. He confidently proclaimed that God would meet the need that night. Then he called for $10,000 commitments, then $20,000. Eventually, a woman raised her hand and pledged the full $100,000 on the spot. Later, she retracted her pledge. She confessed she had felt pressured, not by the Spirit of God but by the pressure coming off the pulpit. A *$profit$* had coerced her in the name of Jesus and that isn't right.

At one of our largest conferences in our church history, the wolf announced that the entire offering would be split between 8 guest ministers, a moment meant to sound generous. That night we raised $800,000 in cash. I know because Kasey and I, along with the false prophetess' sister counted it by hand. It was the largest amount of money I have ever seen. This did not include the money that came in digitally and was never disclosed to us. We were never allowed to see those numbers. Only the wolf and false prophetess had access to the full picture. We were not sure how much or if any money was actually given to each guest minister.

70

This kind of money exchange did not just happen with pastors from other churches; it happened with our staff members as well. I'll be the first to admit to you, I was part of it. You can hate me, rebuke me, or throw stones at me for what I am about to tell you. However, I told you I was going to be completely transparent with you about everything I went through which includes areas in which I was wrong. It's only fair, considering...

I Was Bought at the Price of $90,000

When my wife and I first moved to Tennessee, we were renting, barely making it. The false prophetess pulled us aside and said, *"You should not be renting. It's time for you to own a home."* We agreed but could not afford a down payment. That's when she offered us money. Not a little, a staggering $90,000, which she said was a *"blessing"* from the Lord. We were grateful beyond words until I realized we had been bought with a price. *Thomas*, a staff member who will be mentioned later, had also been given $90,000 for a down payment. Some received money for vehicles, while others were quietly given raises. There was never a board, written record, vote, or accountability. Everyone had a price. Each person's price looked a little different, but the wolf always found out what that price would be and met it. I did not understand nonprofit law back then. I did not know how 501(c)(3)s are required to operate. I surely didn't know the inner workings of the church structure at that point. Looking back, I now realize my loyalty was purchased, not by Christ but by a checkbook. It worked and I felt indebted, tied, and owned. I believed I had been *"blessed,"* when in reality I had been cornered.

The Blessing Became a Burden

When Thomas and I received the $90,000 each, we never saw it as anything other than a blessing or even a miracle. We were told specifically and passionately that we did not need to worry about renting anymore and needed to *own* our homes so we could focus entirely on the ministry God had called us to. The false prophetess looked us in the eyes and said this was God's way of establishing, settling, and positioning us for long-term faithfulness to the vision of the church. We believed her with childlike faith and received those words as encouragement, not manipulation. We never once thought of it as *"taking money from the church."* We saw it as the hand of God making a way where there had been no way. We saw it as provision for the calling we had uprooted our families to pursue and as a supernatural confirmation that the Lord was planting us there. I believed Thomas's heart was pure just as our hearts were. We were simply two families who wanted nothing more than to serve the Lord with all we had. When he received the money for his home, he rejoiced the same way we did, not as men who gained something but as sons who felt seen by God.

Looking back, the emotion is still complex. At the time, it felt like favor, holy affirmation, and blessings the Bible speaks of. This kind of blessing makes you stand still and say, *"Surely God is with us in this place."* We were grateful, humbled, and genuinely believed we were receiving exactly what had been spoken over us, stability for our families, so we could pour ourselves out without reservation. The weight of what we did not know then has hit us now. Our innocence in receiving it was real. Our faith was sincere and gratitude was pure. We did not ask for it or expect it. We did not see it as anything other than the Lord making provision for the ministry that we had willingly given our entire lives to.

Even now, remembering those days evokes a mixture of joy and grief, joy for the purity of heart with which we received it, and grief that something so beautiful was later overshadowed by the reality of how things were handled behind the scenes. I'm so thankful God saw our hearts. Father God knew we received it as sons, never as opportunists or takers but as servants who believed the blessing came from His hand.

The Next Generation Joins the Game

The entanglement did not stop with adults. The wolf's daughter started a for profit T-shirt business. One of our *"house prophets"* offered to donate a huge sum of money but only if she turned the business into a 501(c)(3) nonprofit. He told her it would allow him to donate legally. The girl was barely out of her teens. Her business was 100% for profit. Yet, he pressured her to turn it into a nonprofit just so he could give tax sheltered money. This was not generosity or stewardship. It was spiritual manipulation dressed as *"favor."* Thankfully, she never chose to take that route and eventually closed her business. I want you to clearly understand that I'm ashamed that I did not see it sooner, was part of it, and believed this was *"kingdom partnership."* God showed me the truth, these were not covenants but contracts bought with checks, camouflaged as revival, and upheld by leaders who knew fully well what they were doing.

Revelation

Looking back, I can clearly see what I once thought was favor was really a test and I failed it. What I thought were blessings were actually bondages that later I had to break free from. God, in His mercy, did not leave me bound to broken systems or blinded by loyalty. He began to gently, lovingly, and powerfully show me what His Kingdom truly looks like, and what it never will be. God did not just convict me; He called me higher. He showed me that true spiritual authority is not built through influence, money, charisma, or control. It is formed in humility, holiness, and surrender: *"For thus saith the high and lofty One... I dwell in the high and holy place, with him also that is of a contrite and humble spirit..."* **(Isaiah 57:15 KJV)**. He reminded me that He is not impressed by offerings that are used to build altars to men. He does not applaud leaders who buy loyalty or gather influence through financial manipulation. God searches the heart and weighs motives. He is not mocked. In prayer, the Lord exposed a deeper truth, the Kingdom of God cannot be purchased; the people of God should never be for sale: *"...thy money perish with thee, because thou hast thought that the gift of God may be purchased with money"* **(Acts 8:20 KJV)**. Those words hit me like fire. That is what Simon the Sorcerer attempted to do, buy the power of God for personal influence. Peter rebuked him sharply. I realized then, I had witnessed that same spirit. Even worse, I had enabled it. Perhaps, in some ways I had been blinded by it. God did not show me this to condemn me; He revealed it to redeem me.

Money Disguised as a Blessing for Loyalty

There is a particular grief that comes with realizing generosity was never generosity at all. It is the moment you see that money was not given to bless you but to bind you. That provision came with strings and favor came with expectations. What felt like honor was actually leverage. The pain is not just financial; it is deeply personal. It is the ache of realizing your loyalty was purchased and that your obedience was secured through their provision. Scripture warns us that money has the power to corrupt relationships when it is used to control rather than serve: *"For the love of money is the root of all evil: which while some coveted after, they have erred from the faith, and pierced themselves through with many sorrows"* **(1 Timothy 6:10 KJV)**. When money becomes a tool of influence in spiritual spaces, it pierces not only the giver but the receiver as well. What was meant to help, instead, quietly entangled. This kind of manipulation rarely announces itself as control. It comes dressed as blessing, extra pay, special access, gifts others do not receive, and opportunities framed as favor.

Over time, an unspoken message forms that you are supported because you are aligned. Loyalty is rewarded and silence is subsidized. Distance from leadership suddenly feels financially dangerous. Scripture calls this partiality and it is condemned outright: *"My brethren, have not the faith of our Lord Jesus Christ... with respect of persons"* **(James 2:1 KJV)**.

The realization that you were *"bought"* is humiliating and disorienting. You begin to replay moments in your mind, wondering whether appreciation was genuine or transactional and whether affirmation was spiritual or strategic. It creates shame where there should be none. Scripture places responsibility where it belongs: *"...the borrower is servant to the lender"* **(Proverbs 22:7 KJV)** is not a command; it is a warning. God never intended His people to be bound by financial leverage masquerading as care. When money is used to secure loyalty, truth becomes dangerous. Speaking truthfully risks loss, not just of position but of provision. This is how silence is enforced without ever being demanded. Yet the Word of God is clear, *"You cannot serve God and money"* **(Matthew 6:24 ESV)**.

When financial benefit is tied to obedience to a man rather than obedience to God, mammon has entered the sanctuary. The spiritual damage runs deep. People begin to associate God's blessing with compliance and God's displeasure with independence. Provision becomes conditional, freedom feels irresponsible, and leaving feels like betrayal, not because it is but because the cost has been intentionally made high. Scripture reminds us that God's provision does not depend on human systems: *"The Lord is my shepherd; I shall not want"* **(Psalm 23:1 KJV)**. What God supplies, He does not weaponize.

Healing begins when the lie is exposed; being helped does not mean being owned. Receiving provision does not require forfeiting conscience. Paul refused financial dependence that could compromise his message, saying he would rather labor than allow the gospel to be hindered **(1 Corinthians 9:12 KJV)**. Integrity mattered more than comfort. Healing restores that same clarity, the understanding that freedom in Christ is worth more than any benefit gained by silence. For many, healing also involves forgiving themselves, forgiving the moment you did not see it, the fear that kept you compliant, and confusion that made you stay. God does not condemn you for surviving. He redeems survivors: *"There is therefore now no condemnation for those who are in Christ Jesus"* **(Romans 8:1 ESV)**. You were not weak; you were navigating imbalance of power.

As healing deepens, God gently retrains the heart to trust Him as Provider again. It should not be through manipulation but through faithful care: *"But my God shall supply all your need according to his riches in glory by Christ Jesus"* **(Philippians 4:19 KJV)**. Leaving a system that used money to control does not place you in lack. It places you back under the Shepherd who provides without strings. In time, shame lifts and clarity sharpens. What once felt like betrayal becomes wisdom. You learn that loyalty purchased is not loyalty

76

at all; it is captivity. When Christ sets you free from it, you discover that true blessing never costs your voice, conscience, or obedience to God.

Chapter 5
Leadership Demands Silence
Red Flag: **Silencing the Voices of Opposition**

Truth does not tremble under scrutiny. It does not need to silence its challengers or muzzle its critics. When something is truly born of God it can withstand questions, examination and even opposition because truth carries its own defense, the presence of light. From the beginning of creation, light has never struggled to defeat darkness. It simply appears and darkness disappears. That is the nature of truth. It does not shout to be heard; it shines to be seen. It does not need control to maintain order because truth is its own authority: *"For every one that doeth evil hateth the light, neither cometh to the light, lest his deeds should be reproved. But he that doeth truth cometh to the light, that his deeds may be made manifest, that they are wrought in God"* (*John 3:20–21* KJV).

Jesus Himself made it clear, those who walk in truth come to the light. They have nothing to hide, no need to suppress or silence because their deeds are *"wrought in God."* It is only when deception begins to weave itself into leadership, systems, or hearts that light becomes uncomfortable and truth tellers become threats.

Throughout Scripture the pattern is consistent. When the prophets spoke truth to kings the righteous humbled themselves but the corrupt silenced them. Elijah was hunted by Ahab, Jeremiah was thrown into a pit, and John the Baptist was beheaded for confronting sin. The religious leaders of Jesus' day plotted to kill the very embodiment of truth because His words exposed the motives of their hearts: *"And this is the condemnation, that light is come into the world, and men loved darkness rather than light, because their deeds were evil"* (**John 3:19** KJV).

Even in the house of God, the temptation to protect image can outweigh the call to protect integrity. When fear of exposure replaces the fear of the Lord, the result is always the same; control replaces humility and silence replaces repentance. Truth never asks for silence. Instead, it invites examination, welcomes confession, and can handle questions because truth belongs to God: *"He that walketh uprightly walketh surely: but he that perverteth his ways shall be known"* (**Proverbs 10:9** KJV).

If our walk is upright, we do not have to fear what is revealed. If our hearts are clean, we do not need to guard ourselves against accountability. Only deceit demands secrecy and pride demands silence.

When voices of opposition arise in the Body of Christ, our first instinct should not be to crush them; it should be to listen. Discernment is never developed in an echo chamber. Wisdom does not grow in isolation. The Spirit of God uses correction, counsel, and even confrontation to refine His people. Silencing every voice is to silence the very tool God often uses to keep us from error. Paul wrote to the Corinthians warning them not to glory in men but in the Lord, for *"...the Lord knows the thoughts of the wise, and they are futile"* (**1 Corinthians 3:20** ESV). It is a reminder that human authority is fragile, but divine truth is eternal.

Truth is not afraid of exposure because it *is* exposure, the light of God shining into the hearts of men. When ministries, leaders, or entire systems begin silencing the questions of the faithful, labeling discernment as rebellion or casting correction as attack, it is often a sign that the light has become inconvenient. The Gospel was never meant to be convenient; it was meant to be *cleansing: "For nothing is secret, that shall not be made manifest; neither any thing hid, that shall not be known and come abroad"* **(Luke 8:17 KJV)**. There is a holy confidence in walking transparently before God and man. You don't have to defend what's done in truth or manipulate perception when you are living in the light. The same God who sees in secret rewards openly, both good and evil alike. Truth does not silence opposition. It sanctifies, listens, weighs, and refines because what comes from God will always stand after testing: *"The words of the Lord are pure words: as silver tried in a furnace of earth, purified seven times"* **(Psalm 12:6 KJV)**.

When something must be protected by suppression, it's already in danger of collapse. When it is rooted in God's Word, no criticism can destroy it. The kingdom of God was never meant to be built on silence but on surrender. In every age, God raises voices, prophets, pastors, servants, and sons. It is not to destroy the church but to keep it pure. So, if you find yourself in a place where truth is punished and questioning is forbidden, remember that you are not the problem, darkness is and *"The Light"* will always have the final word.

A Public Apology

I need to take a moment here to apologize, not privately but publicly. There was a time when I participated in something that I now recognize as deeply wrong. It was not done out of hatred or malice, but it was done out of misplaced loyalty. However, that makes it no less serious. At one point during my time on staff, a Facebook group was created about our church. The group grew to nearly 2,500 people, many of them current or former members. Some were angry, hurt, or simply trying to understand what had happened to their friends. Around that same time, my wife Kasey and I

80

were overseeing our church's online ministry platform. Our digital community had nearly 25,000 members who joined weekly for sermons, livestreams, and connection. It was one of the largest parts of our ministry. Then one day, the head of security approached me with a thick stack of papers of Facebook profiles. Each name belonged to someone who was part of that Facebook group. I was told by security that the wolf wanted us to remove them from our online community and block them from our church's official page so that they could not comment, access live services, or *"spread contention."* I was told that these people were being divisive, slandering the church, and enemies of unity. I was also told this was about *"protecting the house."* I obeyed without questioning, prayer, discernment, or compassion. I removed them all, name after name. Some of those people were still attending our services faithfully, being volunteers, and lifelong members. Many of them were not spreading gossip at all; they were simply searching for understanding, trying to make sense of what they or a friend had experienced. I did not take time to question their hearts; I just did my job and followed orders.

In the days that followed, several of them reached out to me personally, confused and hurt, asking why they had been removed. I brought those questions to the wolf and he told me, *"Don't worry about those jokers. Ignore them."* So, I did. At the time, I convinced myself that I was doing the right thing because this is what the wolf told me to do. I was protecting the church, defending leadership, and preserving unity. Now I understand that what I really did was silence the voices of 2,500 people who deserved to be heard. The people who had been hurt by the very ministry I represented were crying out for repentance, healing, and reconciliation. They did not want revenge; they just

wanted to be heard. I helped the wolf take their voice away: *"Therefore, confess your sins to one another and pray for one another, that you may be healed. The prayer of a righteous person has great power as it is working"* (James 5:16 ESV).
I can't undo what I did, but I can repent to God and to them. I deeply apologize to those who were deleted, blocked, or ignored. I silenced your pain because I did not know how to sit with it. I justified your removal in the name of order, when I should have chosen the way of Christ by listening, loving, and repenting. Kasey and I reached out to some of you later, trying to apologize. I remember being told, *"You're just on an apology tour,"* as if our remorse was performative. I understood why you felt the way you did. We had spent so long defending a system that had hurt people that any repentance seemed suspicious. Our repentance was genuine and it still is today.
I now realize something that took me years to see; you should not delete people just because they disagree with you. You should not block the broken and call it discernment or mute the hurting and call it unity. We serve a God of reconciliation, not removal. Jesus, our Savior leaves the ninety-nine for the one: *"And all things are of God, who hath reconciled us to himself by Jesus Christ, and hath given to us the ministry of reconciliation"* (2 Corinthians 5:18 KJV).
Kasey and I failed to represent that heart. The wolf and false prophetess failed to hear those who had been wounded by their decisions. They failed to seek reconciliation; I failed to speak up when I should have stood for what was right. If you're reading this and you were among those I blocked, ignored, or dismissed, I want you to know, I hear you now, I see you now, and I repent for being a part of silencing you.

The church was never meant to be a place where questions are punished and pain is hidden. It's supposed to be like a hospital for the hurting, not a courtroom for the broken. I don't want to be an agent of pain anymore. I want to be an agent of healing, the very hands and feet of the Lord Jesus. He listened to the outcast, restored the fallen, and washed the feet of the very ones who would deny Him. If I can offer any small redemption through this confession, please know that repentance is real and healing is possible. Even those who once silenced you can find their voice again, not to defend what was done but to declare that grace is greater than shame: *"The LORD is near to the brokenhearted and saves the crushed in spirit"* (**Psalm 34:18** ESV). I am one of them.

What Silence Teaches

When I look back at that season, the Facebook group, deleted names, and voices I silenced, I no longer see it as an isolated mistake but as a mirror. It is a mirror that reflects back to me just how easy it is to defend a system instead of the Savior and how quickly good intentions can become blind obedience when truth takes a back seat to loyalty.

At the time, I thought I was protecting the church. However, the Lord has since shown me that the church does not need protection from people; it needs purification before Him. I thought I was defending unity, but I was really preserving comfort. Comfort can become an idol when it keeps you from confronting what's wrong. God has used this moment to open my eyes to what true leadership, repentance, and reconciliation look like in the *Kingdom*: *"And we know that all things work together for good to them that love God, to them who are the called according to his purpose"* (**Romans 8:28** KJV).

The enemy meant to shame me, bury me under guilt, and convince me that my failure had disqualified my calling. God in His mercy has taken that same failure and turned it into a classroom. He has shown me that the moment we stop listening to the cries of His people, we stop representing His heart. Jesus did not silence those who were hurting; He drew near to them. He did not block their questions; He answered them. When I silenced those voices, I silenced a part of His heart and that realization broke me. It was in that breaking that revelation began to come: *"For God, who commanded the light to shine out of darkness, hath shined in our hearts, to give the light of the knowledge of the glory of God in the face of Jesus Christ"* **(2 Corinthians 4:6 KJV)**. I began to understand that what the enemy used to darken my discernment, God was now using to ignite my compassion. The very thing I did wrong became the tool God used to teach me how to love rightly. He taught me that no one is disposable in the Kingdom. Not one name on that list was *"just another person."* Each one was a soul He bled for, had a story, and mattered. When I crossed their names off a list, I was crossing out the very ones Jesus would have left the ninety-nine to go find. That realization undid me. That is the beauty of repentance, it does not leave you in ruin, but it rebuilds you with revelation. God did not just forgive me; He gave me understanding. That understanding has now changed everything about how I lead, love, and see people. I used to think leadership meant guarding the platform, but it means washing feet. I thought unity meant silence, but it means sincerity: *"He hath shewed thee, O man, what is good; and what doth the LORD require of thee, but to do justly, and to love mercy, and to walk humbly with thy God?"* **(Micah 6:8 KJV)**. The Lord has shown me living justly means telling the truth even when it hurts. Loving mercy means forgiving those who hurt you and asking forgiveness from those you have hurt. Walking humbly means staying long enough to hear both God and people. The Lord took my failure and turned it into my greatest teacher. I have learned that redemption does not erase the past, it redeems it. He's used this story to awaken something in me, a new conviction, compassion, and a calling to be a voice for those who have been silenced: *"As for you, you meant evil against me, but God meant it for good, to bring it about that many people should be kept alive, as they are today"* **(Genesis 50:20 ESV)**.

The enemy thought this moment would ruin me and shame would keep me silent forever. God turned it into an altar, a place where I could finally lay down pride, image, and control and find freedom in simply being truthful. I see now that repentance is not weakness; it is warfare. Every time we tell the truth, we strip the enemy of his power. When we humble ourselves the Spirit of God draws nearer. Every time we stop defending what's broken and start rebuilding what's holy, heaven rejoices. God has used this to teach me that *"restoration always begins where truth is told."* The truth is, I was wrong, silenced people I should have listened to, and misrepresented the heart of Christ. He has forgiven me and using my story to help others find their own freedom.

This experience taught me that ministry is about keeping things clean; it's about keeping hearts close to the Father. The church is not preserved by image management but by humble repentance. Now when I think about those 2,500 names, I no longer feel shame. I feel burdened but in a holy way because I know that for every person I once silenced there are thousands more who need to hear that God still heals, restores, brings beauty from ashes, and purpose from pain: *"The LORD is gracious, and full of compassion; slow to anger, and of great mercy"* **(Psalm 145:8 KJV)**. What the enemy meant to:

- use to divide, God has used to unite
- shame me, God has used to shape me
- silence, God has turned into a song of redemption

Now, I speak not as a man defending myself but as one who has been delivered. The very voice I once used to silence others now has been redeemed by God to speak freedom. I will spend the rest of my days using it for the purpose of protecting, reconciling, and reminding the church that truth and love are not enemies, they are the evidence of Jesus living among us.

Silence That Was Not God's Will

There is a silence that is holy and there is a silence that is coerced. One is rooted in wisdom; the other is rooted in fear. When leadership demands silence to protect power, preserve image, or avoid accountability, that silence becomes a form of violence against the soul. It suppresses truth, fractures conscience, and slowly teaches the people of God to confuse obedience with self-betrayal. Scripture never treats enforced silence as righteousness. God repeatedly condemns leaders who silence truth to protect themselves: *"Woe to those who call evil good and good evil, who put darkness for light and light for darkness..."* **(Isaiah 5:20 ESV)**. When leaders demand silence in the face of wrongdoing, they are not guarding unity, they are inverting morality. The people who comply are left carrying a weight they were never meant to bear.

Many believers live with deep regret over the words they swallowed, moments they froze, and truth they knew but did not speak. That regret often turns inward as shame, *"I should have known better. I should have spoken up. I failed God."* God rebukes shepherds who scatter the sheep and declare, *"My people have been lost sheep: their shepherds have caused them to go astray..."* **(Jeremiah 50:6 KJV)**. Silence learned under pressure is not moral failure; it is survival within a system designed to suppress truth. Leadership that demands silence often spiritualizes it. You are told it is for *"unity, covering, or protecting the anointing."* Biblical unity is never built on secrecy or fear. The apostle Paul publicly confronted Peter before them all when the truth of the gospel was compromised **(Galatians 2:11–14 KJV)**. Silence would have preserved peace, but it would have corrupted truth. Scripture makes it clear that peace purchased by silence is not peace at all.

When voices are silenced, the conscience suffers. Over time, believers begin to distrust their own discernment. They learn to ignore the inner witness of the Spirit in order to stay safe. Yet the Word of God commands the opposite: *"Open your mouth for the mute, for the rights of all who are destitute"* **(Proverbs 31:8 ESV)**. God does not anoint silence that allows harm to continue. He calls His people to speak for those who cannot. The cost of enforced silence is heavy. Truth unspoken does not disappear; it turns inward, manifests as anxiety, depression, spiritual numbness, and physical exhaustion. David described this agony when he said, *"When I kept silence, my bones waxed old through my roaring all the day long"* **(Psalm 32:3 KJV)**. Silence demanded by fear erodes the soul because it violates how God designed truth to function, speak, confess, and bring it to the light.

Healing begins with repentance, not for speaking too much but for believing the lie that silence was obedience. Jesus never praised those who protected systems at the expense of truth. He said plainly, *"For there is nothing covered, that shall not be revealed; neither hid, that shall not be known"* **(Luke 12:2 KJV)**. Truth does not require permission to surface. You are not condemned for the time it took you to see that. Restoring your voice is a process, not a performance. Scripture says, *"...the righteous are bold as a lion"* **(Proverbs 28:1 ESV)**, but boldness grows over time as trust is rebuilt. You do not have to say everything to everyone. Wisdom still matters but silence that once came from fear must be replaced with obedience to God rather than men: *"...We must obey God rather than men"* **(Acts 5:29 ESV)**.

As healing deepens, the Holy Spirit retrains your discernment. You learn the difference between peace and avoidance, between humility and suppression. The fear that once kept you quiet loses its grip: *"For God hath not given us the spirit of fear; but of power, and of love, and of a sound mind"* **(2 Timothy 1:7 KJV)**. The voice God restores is not reckless. It is clear, grounded, and anchored in truth. The final stage of healing is releasing the shame of delayed obedience. Scripture reminds us, *"There is therefore now no condemnation to them which are in Christ Jesus..."* **(Romans 8:1 KJV)**. God redeems not only what was spoken but what was withheld. When your voice returns, it is not to tear down indiscriminately but to bear witness to truth with wisdom and love.

Silence demanded by leadership was never your calling. You were not created to protect darkness or absorb injustice quietly. You were created to walk in the light. When God restores your voice, it becomes testimony, not of failure but of deliverance.

Chapter 6
Apostolic Covering
Red Flag: **Self Appointed Title Holders**

Throughout Scripture, God establishes order within His Church so His people may flourish in faith, unity, and purpose. One of the most misunderstood aspects of that divine order is what many call apostolic covering. It is a term that carries great weight but is often used with little understanding. In its truest form, apostolic covering is not about hierarchy, control, or personal authority; it is about spiritual care, accountability, and equipping. It reflects the heart of God who never leaves His people uncovered or unguarded. From the earliest days of the church, the Lord raised up apostles to establish foundations of truth, guide new believers, and ensure that everything built upon the Gospel would remain strong and sound. Their leadership was not self-appointed nor was it self-serving. It was marked by humility, tested by obedience, and confirmed by fruit. Understanding apostolic covering biblically requires us to return to the Word, not to cultural definitions, denominational structures, or modern titles but to the pattern laid out in Scripture. For only in the Word can we rediscover the beauty of leadership that both protects and empowers the people of God: *"And he gave some, apostles; and some, prophets; and some, evangelists; and some, pastors and teachers; For the perfecting of the saints, for the work of the ministry, for the edifying of the body of Christ"* **(Ephesians 4:11–12 KJV).**

Apostolic covering, biblically defined, is first about function, not title. Christ Himself distributes ministry gifts for a purpose to:

- mature believers (perfecting of the saints)
- mobilize them into service (the work of the ministry)
- strengthen the whole church (edifying of the body)

Within this framework, the apostle's role is catalytic and equipping. The apostolic grace does not terminate on the apostle; it flows through the apostle to shape healthy doctrine, raise competent leaders, and release believers into calling with courage and clarity. Where this grace operates you will see saints become stable, skillful, scripturally rooted, ministries taking shape with order and integrity, and the entire body experiencing growth in unity, not dependency on one person. When God's design is working, the church grows strong. Believers mature, ministry is shared, and Jesus stays at the center. When leadership creates fear, control, or dependence, something has drifted from God's plan. Apostolic leadership is meant to build, not control. Like a builder, apostles lay a strong foundation, teach others, and then step back so God's people can grow. The Bible says the church is built on the foundation of the apostles and prophets, with Jesus as the cornerstone (*Ephesians 2:20* KJV). The foundation matters but it stays low and the center of focus is Jesus. True authority builds people up. Paul said authority is given for edification, not destruction (*2 Corinthians 10:8* ESV). Healthy leaders strengthen faith, encourage growth, and point people to Christ, not to themselves. The Bible calls leaders shepherds, not rulers. They lead by example, not force (*1 Peter 5:2–3* KJV). They welcome accountability, protect sound teaching, and serve with humility. Jesus said the greatest leaders are servants (*Matthew 23:11* ESV).

In 2024, our church experienced a significant milestone. The wolf was ordained as an apostle in a beautiful and heartfelt ceremony that the false prophetess had organized as a surprise for his birthday. Leaders and friends from partnering ministries gathered to celebrate the moment. The atmosphere was filled with joy, honor, and anticipation for what God would do next. I was fully supportive and genuinely moved by the ordination. It felt like a turning point for our church launching into something greater and a new chapter that would expand our reach and deepen our mission.

The wolf had often spoken about being called to the nations, and as part of the staff, we were eager to come alongside that calling. We believed the Lord was broadening the vision. Apostolic ministry, after all, is about reaching beyond the walls and carrying the name of Jesus to new territories.

Over time, a quiet shift began to take place in the structure of leadership. The wolf became increasingly hands off with day-to-day operations. Meetings and ministry details began to flow through the false prophetess, who stepped naturally into a more active leadership role. Eventually, staff meetings proceeded without his attendance. Though he would occasionally be present, he rarely spoke and the ongoing oversight of ministry matters rested entirely with her.

During this same period, the wolf began traveling frequently to Israel. By the end of 2024, he had taken more than thirty trips and the visits continued in 2025. Each trip was described as ministry work involvement in projects within the land of Israel. However, there has been very little communication about what that work involved or how it connected to our church's mission. The false prophetess mentioned that some of his activities are covered by nondisclosure agreements which prevent public discussion. We respected that boundary, yet the absence of clear information naturally left many uncertain about the details.

One of the most notable moments came when the wolf made a personal donation of $90,000 to the Red Heifer Program in Israel. The contribution was presented as an act of support for biblical prophecy and Israel's future. While the generosity was unquestioned, the process lacked transparency. There was no board consultation or public explanation of how that decision was made. Scripture emphasizes that financial stewardship in ministry should be handled with openness and integrity, not for suspicion's sake, but for protection: *"Providing for honest things, not only in the sight of the Lord, but also in the sight of men"* (**2 Corinthians 8:21 KJV**). Paul's words remind us that transparency is not a matter of distrust; it is a safeguard. It honors both God and His people. When financial decisions are made openly, they inspire confidence and protect the integrity of the ministry. Stewardship without shared accountability can unintentionally create confusion, even when motives are pure. The biblical standard protects everyone involved such as the givers, receivers, and reputation of the Gospel itself.

Beyond financial matters, the wolf's close relationships with various Rabbis in Israel also drew attention. As believers, we absolutely stand with Israel both scripturally and morally. The Lord's covenant with His people is eternal and our responsibility is to pray for and bless the nation that has given us the Messiah. Yet the Scriptures also remind us that partnership in ministry must remain rooted in the confession of Christ: *"And there is salvation in no one else, for there is no other name under heaven given among men by which we must be saved"* (**Acts 4:12 ESV**).

When Peter stood before the religious leaders of his day, he boldly declared the name of Jesus, knowing it could cost him everything. The power of the Gospel has always been in the Name, the only name that heals, redeems, and saves. I do not share this to criticize anyone's approach but to affirm what Scripture has solidified in my own conviction. The message of Christ loses its power when His name is withheld. In addition, the wolf has spoken openly about his involvement in discussions surrounding the rebuilding of the Third Temple and mentioned hopes of participating in ceremonies connected to it. On one of his podcasts, he referred to the red heifer sacrifices as *"ceremonies,"* explaining that he used that term out of respect for rabbinical sensitivities. We can stand with Israel politically and prophetically while still affirming that redemption is found in Christ alone.

As these developments unfolded, one consistent pattern became clear. Our church's apostolic structure has not reflected the biblical rhythm of building, planting, and multiplying. The wolf continues to evangelize in various regions, but there has not been a clear effort to establish churches, disciple local pastors, or strategically plant ministries where the gospel can take deeper root. Apostolic leadership, biblically speaking, is both *evangelistic* and *architectural;* it reaches and it builds: *"According to the grace of God which is given unto me, as a wise masterbuilder, I have laid the foundation, and another buildeth thereon"* **(1 Corinthians 3:10 KJV).**

The apostolic gift is meant to extend beyond preaching tours and personal ministry engagements; it carries the responsibility to construct spiritual infrastructure, churches, teams, and local leaders who can continue the work. Without that, the movement becomes dependent on a single voice rather than multiplying the message of Christ.

Equally important is the inward work of strengthening the congregation already entrusted to an apostolic leader. Scripture reveals that apostles not only planted churches but continually nurtured them. Paul revisited cities, wrote letters, sent trusted co-laborers, and maintained active care for the believers he served. Apostolic ministry that neglects the spiritual health of its home base loses half of its divine purpose: *"shepherd the flock of God that is among you, exercising oversight, not under compulsion, but willingly, ... not domineering over those in your charge, but being examples to the flock"* (**1 Peter 5:2–3 ESV**). This verse captures the balance of biblical oversight, leadership that watches, feeds, and models godliness. Apostolic calling includes both the nations abroad and the people within. The Lord has reminded me repeatedly that mission begins at home. Stewardship always starts with the flock already entrusted before reaching for broader influence: *"Moreover it is required in stewards, that a man be found faithful"* (**1 Corinthians 4:2 KJV**).

Stewardship is a mirror

When the wolf began calling himself an *apostle*, he told the church that God had entrusted him with assignments too great for ordinary leaders. One of those assignments, he claimed, was the collection of rare biblical artifacts such as ancient scroll fragments, pottery from biblical eras, Nazi era historical pieces, and even items connected to C. H. Spurgeon. He said he had spent hundreds of thousands of dollars, maybe millions to acquire them and that they would one day be displayed in his bible museum to teach nations and strengthen the faith of our congregation. At first, it sounded noble, even sacred. Over time, what began as excitement slowly revealed the truth, the fruit did not match the title. What I watched unfold did not reflect the fruit of apostleship, it revealed something much more concerning.

The artifacts were constantly talked about but never stewarded. They sat in his office like trophies on a shelf, shown only to select people as if they were private proof of his spiritual importance. He promised the congregation they would soon see everything but that unveiling never came. When we transitioned into our new building, it would have made sense to protect these irreplaceable objects and move toward the museum he had spoken of, but the opposite happened. Quietly and without explanation, the artifacts were hauled to an on-site building that had no electricity, climate control, security, or proper protection. Thousands of years of history, scrolls that had survived persecution and war, pottery preserved through centuries, and Spurgeon artifacts saturated with revival history were now stacked in cardboard boxes in the dark, left to decay. What once was presented as sacred was now treated with shocking carelessness. It was in that moment that everything became clear. A true apostle does not mishandle what he calls holy. The Apostle Paul said, *"Moreover it is required in stewards that one be found faithful"* (**1 Corinthians 4:2 KJV**). Faithful stewardship is not optional for spiritual leaders; it is the sign of genuine calling. What I saw was not stewardship, but negligence disguised as vision. It was an image of apostolic greatness without the substance of apostolic responsibility. When someone claims God entrusted them with something but then treats it recklessly, the issue is not only the artifact but also the condition of the heart. Scripture says plainly, *"One who is faithful in a very little is also faithful in much, and one who is dishonest in a very little is also dishonest in much"* (**Luke 16:10 ESV**). If a man cannot faithfully steward physical things, why should anyone believe that he can steward spiritual ones?

What made this even more painful was that these artifacts were not collected for ministry, they were collected for image. They were bought loudly and stored poorly. They were promoted publicly and neglected privately. This disconnect revealed a truth I did not want to see; he wanted the appearance of an apostolic calling, not the accountability of one. Real apostles build people, protect the sacred, and equip the saints. False apostles thrive on private collections, discard the sacred, and hoard what God meant for His Church. However here, sacred things were hidden, mishandled, and left to rot. The people who were promised access were never given it. The apostle Paul said, *"But we have renounced the hidden things of shame... but by manifestation of the truth commending ourselves to every man's conscience in the sight of God"* **(2 Corinthians 4:2 NKJV).**

Apostolic ministry is transparent, but darkness reveals an entirely different spirit at work. The museum that never surfaced became its own kind of revelation. It exposed a painful and undeniable truth that when a leader elevates his title above his character, everything entrusted to him begins to decay physically and spiritually. Stewardship is not just about managing resources; it is about honoring God with what we claim is His. The careless handling of these artifacts was not merely a logistical failure; it was a spiritual warning. It showed that the title *apostle* meant more to him than the fruit of apostleship, what God calls sacred had become a prop, and accountability had been replaced with ego. Scripture warns us plainly, *"If the foundations are destroyed, what can the righteous do?"* **(Psalm 11:3 NKJV).** When the foundation of stewardship collapses, everything built on it eventually follows. In the end, the museum was not just a failed project; it was a mirror. A mirror that:

- revealed what happened when a man claimed spiritual authority he could not uphold
- showed how far a leader could drift when his title became more important than his obedience
- exposed the difference between a man appointed by God and a man appointed by his own ambition

Once you see it, you cannot unsee it. The artifacts in those boxes preached a sermon louder than any spoken from the stage; titles can be claimed, sermons can be crafted, but the way a man handles sacred things reveals the truth about his heart. In that dim unprotected storage room, the truth became impossible to ignore.

Titles that Bear Weight

As I continued to observe the unfolding of ministry life within our church, the Lord began to teach me something deeper about titles and responsibility. It became clear to me that while a title may identify an office, only character and obedience can confirm the call. Titles themselves hold no anointing, obedience does. The Bible never separates position from purpose, nor authority from accountability. When we pursue the recognition of a title more than the reflection of Christ, we trade divine commission for human ambition.

Paul wrote in **(Ephesians 4:1 KJV)**, *"I therefore, the prisoner of the Lord, beseech you that ye walk worthy of the vocation wherewith ye are called."* The word *vocation* here means *"calling,"* but it is not limited to occupation or office. It is a summons to live in harmony with what God has entrusted. Walking worthy means walking weight-bearing. Every title in Scripture carries a cross, not a crown of convenience. The higher the title, the heavier the responsibility. To wear one rightly is to kneel under it in humility and dependence upon the

97

Holy Spirit. In today's culture, we often celebrate the title but neglect the transformation required to sustain it. Yet the Word of God outlines clear expectations for each office, each one intertwined with holiness, integrity, and servanthood. When those expectations are ignored, the position itself becomes hollow and leadership drifts into self-appointment rather than divine commission. Jesus warned of this very danger: *"Not every one that saith unto me, Lord, Lord, shall enter into the kingdom of heaven; but he that doeth the will of my Father which is in heaven"* **(Matthew 7:21 KJV)**. The difference between calling and counterfeiting is obedience.

The apostle Paul never gloried in his title but in his servanthood. He called himself *"...a servant of Jesus Christ, called to be an apostle"* **(Romans 1:1 NKJV)**. Notice the order, servant first, apostle second. Servanthood qualifies leadership. Without it, titles become self-exalting rather than Christ exalting. True biblical authority flows from submission, first to Christ, then to His Word, and finally to the accountability of His people. Authority detached from submission becomes tyranny, but authority rooted in surrender becomes blessing.

The Spirit of God, through Paul, was showing that titles cannot be assigned lightly. They must rest on shoulders that have been seasoned through humility and tested through faithfulness. Promotion in the Kingdom is never positional, it's transformational. God does not promote gifts; He promotes character. Likewise, the prophet Jeremiah confronted a generation of leaders who claimed divine authority without divine appointment: *"I have not sent these prophets, yet they ran: I have not spoken to them, yet they prophesied"* **(Jeremiah 23:21 KJV)**. This sobering verse reveals that spiritual activity without divine instruction is rebellion

98

disguised as zeal. When we move ahead of God's voice, we begin to operate in the flesh while using His name. It may sound spiritual, but it lacks the substance of Scripture and the seal of the Holy Spirit.

I began to see that titles alone cannot validate a ministry, fruit does. Jesus said, *"Ye shall know them by their fruits"* (**Matthew 7:16 KJV**). The fruit of true leaders demonstrate sound doctrine, equip believers, feed and protect the sheep, and speak words that align with the written Word and glorify Christ. Every biblical title has a corresponding assignment that can be measured by the fruit it bears. Titles for the sake of recognition lead to spiritual imbalance. When we crave the affirmation of a name rather than the affirmation of heaven, we become susceptible to deception. The church in Sardis carried a reputation of being alive, but the Lord said, *"I know your works. You have the reputation of being alive, but you are dead"* (**Revelation 3:1 ESV**). It is possible to have a name, even a spiritual one, yet lack the life of the Holy Spirit. A title cannot resurrect what obedience has left buried. God's design for leadership has never changed. Every role is meant to reflect the nature of Christ including the:

- apostle who was sent
- prophet who spoke truth
- evangelist who proclaimed good news
- pastor who shepherded His flock
- teacher who revealed the Father's heart

To hold any of these offices is to carry a portion of His ministry on earth. The standard is so high because the reflection must be holy: *"...BE YE HOLY; FOR I AM HOLY"* (**1 Peter 1:16 KJV**).

As I watched these truths unfold within our own church, the Lord convicted me personally. It is not enough to recognize imbalance; we must respond by embodying the biblical pattern ourselves. Whether we hold a title or not, we are all called to walk worthy of the calling of Christ. It is far better to live with no title and full obedience than to bear a title without fruit. Paul summarized this so powerfully: *"For though ye have ten thousand instructors in Christ, yet have ye not many fathers..."* **(1 Corinthians 4:15 KJV)**. The church does not need more titles; it needs more fathers and mothers in the faith, leaders who carry the heart of Christ, and the weight of responsibility that comes with representing Him. When we return to the biblical blueprint, titles regain their beauty. They stop demanding recognition and start producing fruit. They reflect the nature of the One who *"But made himself of no reputation, and took upon him the form of a servant..."* **(Philippians 2:7 KJV)**. Bearing a title without the corresponding burden of service is like holding a crown we have not earned. True apostolic order is to walk humbly, faithfully, and scripturally in the office God has called us. Titles will pass away, but obedience will echo through eternity.

The Phone Call that Shook Me

There are moments in ministry you never shake. Moments that mark you and open your eyes so sharply you realize something is terribly wrong. I was answering the church phone, an ordinary task I had done countless times. The phone rang and the caller ID showed an international Israeli number. I hesitated, not wanting to risk unnecessary charges, letting the phone ring and go to voicemail. At the time, it felt insignificant and routine. That changed the moment I listened to the message. The caller was cold, calculated, and unrestrained. It was not just a voicemail; it was a demand and warning from an Israeli Rabbi stating the agreement was not fulfilled and had to be done from the pulpit in front of his congregation and online viewers. It was like a spiritual earthquake. The voice on the other end carried a fury I had never heard before. The Rabbi's message made it unmistakably clear that agreements had not been met and consequences were imminent if immediate compliance did not follow. The demands were precise, the timeline urgent, and the tone left no room for misunderstanding. Then the message turned even darker. What followed was not instruction, correction, or reconciliation, but leverage. Accusations were spoken with chilling confidence, the kind that assumes power has already been secured. The caller revealed devastating information regarding the wolf and demanded his obedience rather than dialogue. He sounded like someone prepared to destroy lives if defied; was this blackmail? I stood there holding the church phone with my stomach in knots. No one prepares you for moments like that. Ministry is supposed to be about shepherding, prayer, and compassion, not intimidation, coercion, fear or threats that make your blood run cold. When the voicemail ended, I did not move. I did not know who to tell or what to think. One thing became very clear; involving someone outside the organization in this way was intentional. It created pressure, leverage, and fear and nothing about it felt holy. Nothing about it bore the fruit of righteous leadership.

Then Sunday came and in the middle of an otherwise unrelated sermon, without context or explanation, everything shifted. The tone changed, the urgency sharpened, and right there in front of the entire congregation, the wolf said exactly what the voicemail had demanded. This theatrical performance by the wolf was precise. The puppet master was obviously in control. It wasn't pure or Spirit-led, not even connected to the message being preached. It was compliance, word for word. My heart dropped, my palms began to sweat, and my pulse raced as I witnessed the orchestrated performance by the wolf. I felt physically ill, as though the ground beneath me was no longer stable. I had heard the threat, I knew the demand, and I was watching it being obeyed from the pulpit as though it were obedience to God. I never received another call like that; I did not need one either. That single moment revealed a hidden world beneath the surface of our church, a world of private arrangements, unseen pressures, unspoken leverage, and fear driven obedience. It exposed a layer of darkness I never expected to encounter in ministry and forced me to confront a truth I did not want to face. When a pulpit becomes a place where threats are obeyed instead of God's Word, the fall has already begun long before the collapse becomes public. That call was more than a warning; it was a revelation. From that moment on, I knew everything was not as it appeared; I knew I had to get out. In present day, after the phone call and public declaration, the wolf has now added an accountability partner, the jester, to travel the world with him. Apostolic leadership was never meant to look like what I witnessed. It was never meant to be defined by titles claimed, artifacts collected, private agreements made, or threats obeyed. In Scripture, apostles were men who:

- were humble
- washed feet
- protected the flock
- laid down their lives
- feared God far more than they feared exposure

The more I walked through these experiences watching sacred things mishandled, authority used as a shield, and the pulpit respond to threats instead of the Holy Spirit, I realized how far from biblical apostleship I had drifted. The apostle Paul wrote, *"For we do not preach ourselves, but Christ Jesus the Lord, and ourselves your bondservants for Jesus' sake"* **(2 Corinthians 4:5 NKJV)**. Somewhere along the way, the message shifted. It was no longer Christ preached, servanthood, or stewardship. It had become man elevated, control, and secrecy. True apostolic leadership carries weight; but it is the weight of responsibility, not the weight of dominance. It carries authority, but it is authority used to lift others, not build oneself up. It carries revelation but revelation aligned with Scripture, not imaginations crafted in private. It is marked by humility, accountability, and transparency. Anything else is imitation, not inheritance. That was the hardest realization of all; the title of apostle does not make a man apostolic. The fruit does. Jesus said plainly, *"Even so, every good tree bears good fruit... every tree is known by its own fruit"* **(Matthew 7:17; Luke 6:44 NKJV)**. What I had seen was neglect, fear, threats, manipulation, inconsistency, and hiddenness; it was truly witchcraft. So, the Lord taught me something I never expected to learn in ministry; a title can be claimed, a platform can be built, and a following can be gathered. However, apostolic leadership is proven only by the fear of the Lord and the fruit of righteousness. When the fruit is missing, the title becomes a fast-food paper crown, *"Have it your way."* It eventually collapses. This chapter does not end with accusation but ends with clarity, not man's way but God's way. It was clarity for me and no longer confusion. Once the Lord opens your eyes to what true apostleship looks like, you are no longer blind.

Self-Appointed Title Holders
Leaders use their titles as shields against correction and weapons against discernment. Questioning them is framed as questioning God. Disagreement is labeled

rebellion. The Scriptures never support this. Even Paul, who was genuinely called by God, consistently defended his apostleship by pointing to fruit, suffering, and sacrifice, not by demanding recognition **(2 Corinthians 12:12 KJV)**. True authority never needs to announce itself. The damage caused by self-appointed title holders is subtle but severe. Believers begin to doubt their own standing with God. They feel spiritually inferior, dependent, and disqualified. Access to God feels mediated through the *"anointed one."* Scripture dismantles this illusion completely: *"But you are a chosen generation, a royal priesthood..."* **(1 Peter 2:9 NKJV)**.

Self-appointed leaders often appeal to mystery. *"You would not understand, this is above your level, and God deals with me differently."* Scripture says the opposite: *"The secret things belong unto the LORD our God: but those things which are revealed belong unto us and to our children for ever..."* **(Deuteronomy 29:29 KJV)**. Many were taught that leaving a self-appointed authority would result in spiritual exposure or judgment. Scripture reminds us, *"The LORD is your keeper..."* **(Psalm 121:5 KJV)**. Christ does not outsource protection of His sheep. You were never under a man's covering; you were always under God's care. Believers learn to test callings rather than assume them. Scripture instructs us not to receive claims of spiritual authority blindly, *"Let the prophets speak two or three, and let the other judge"* **(1 Corinthians 14:29 KJV)**. Authority in the Kingdom is confirmed in community, not declared in isolation. You will recognize true leaders by their fruit. Jesus said plainly, *"Wherefore by their fruits ye shall know them"* **(Matthew 7:20 KJV)**.

Chapter 7
Lies to Generate Tithes

The God Who Sees in Secret
From Genesis to Revelation, Scripture reveals a God who is not merely aware of the hidden things of the human heart, He is the God who exposes them. Nothing escapes His gaze. There is no corner of the sanctuary, whispered conversation, hidden motive, or secret practice that stands outside the light of His presence. The Lord who walked with Adam in the cool of the day is the same Lord who *"...searches all hearts and understands all the intent of the thoughts"* (**1 Chronicles 28:9 NKJV**). Before we step into the stories, hurts, or realities that follow in this chapter, we must first anchor ourselves in what God Himself declares about truth, darkness, and revelation.

Darkness vs. Light
The Bible never treats darkness as powerful, only deceptive. Darkness is simply the absence of light and wherever the light of God shines, the shadows flee. Jesus said, *"For nothing is hidden that will not be made manifest, nor is anything secret that will not be known and come to light"* (**Luke 8:17 ESV**). With those words, He established a kingdom principle. Truth has a destiny and hidden things have an appointment with exposure. It is not a rare disruption to the normal order; it *is* the order. Darkness does not delay truth. It only multiplies the force of its revelation. Paul wrote to the church, *"Take no part in the unfruitful works of darkness, but instead expose them"* (**Ephesians 5:11 ESV**). Notice the mandate not to tolerate, excuse, or ignore but expose.

Why? Because hidden works rot from the inside out. A ministry may produce noise, crowds, programs, events, and emotion but if its foundation contains hidden corruption, none of it will stand. Jesus Himself declared that every tree not planted by His Father would be *"rooted up"* **(Matthew 15:13 ESV)**. Exposure is God's uprooting and His divine refusal to allow His people to be nourished by contaminated vines.

The Guardrail Against Secret Corruption

Scripture teaches that the *"fear of the Lord is clean, enduring for ever..."* **(Psalm 19:9 KJV)**. Wherever the fear of the Lord is absent, hidden works multiply. Wherever the fear of the Lord is present, even secret places become sanctified. The fear of the Lord is not terror; it is the awareness that God is near, watching, and will judge rightly. It is the realization that we minister before the God who told Jeremiah, *"Can a man hide himself in secret places so that I cannot see him?...Do I not fill heaven and earth?..."* **(Jeremiah 23:24 ESV)**. In healthy ministries, this awareness produces integrity, humility, and transparency. In unhealthy ministries, especially those built around personality, performance, and platform, this awareness becomes inconvenient. What is inconvenient to the flesh soon becomes ignored, then resisted and silenced until darkness becomes normal. Darkness is expelled in the kingdom of God.

Pattern of Exposure

The Bible is a book of repeated exposures, not because God delights in revealing sin but because He refuses to allow hidden sin to dominate His people. Achan tried to hide stolen items beneath his tent **(Joshua 7 KJV)**. What one man buried, God uncovered. David tried to hide his sin with Bathsheba (*2 Samuel 11–12* KJV). What a king concealed, God confronted through a prophet. Ananias and Sapphira hid their deception beneath *"generosity"* (*Acts 5* ESV). What they pretended to offer, God exposed in the presence of the church. The Pharisees cloaked their greed and hypocrisy in religious garments (*Matthew 23* ESV). What they polished on the outside, Jesus illuminated from within. The pattern is always the same. Things people hide, cover, and manipulate are revealed, uncovered and judged by God. Exposure is not God's punishment; it is His mercy, protection, and commitment to truth. There can be no:

- healing without revealing
- restoration without repentance
- righteousness where sin abides

Confronting Broken Promises

The matter of promises made publicly in the house of God but never kept should be addressed. We will address fundraisers that stirred excitement, inspired giving, and moved the hearts of generous people. Yet the projects themselves were never built, never planned, and in many cases never progressed beyond a spoken idea. Money was collected for visions that never had blueprints. Dreams were cast that never had foundations. Offerings were taken for *"what is coming,"* even when nothing was being prepared behind the scenes. This is not written to condemn but to call to repentance, not repentance before man alone but repentance before God. Look at Zacchaeus and see what true repentance looks like, not only is it verbal but it is necessary to restore. It costs more to sin than to live righteous. Scripture warns us that *"...it is required in stewards, that a man be found faithful"* (*1 Corinthians 4:2* KJV). When leaders mishandle trust, whether through neglect, deception, or carelessness, they do not simply violate organizational ethics, they violate the fear of the Lord. Earthly courts may address violations of law, but the courts of heaven address violations of the heart. Earthly consequences are temporary; eternal judgments are not. Jesus Himself taught plainly: *"But let your communication be, Yea, yea; Nay, nay..."* **(Matthew 5:37 KJV)**. Lying to people and using their resources is not a small matter. This is not about lawsuits or penalties. This is about integrity, holiness, and standing before the Lord with clean hands and a pure heart **(Psalm 24:3–4 KJV)**. We are searing our conscience **(1 Timothy 4:2 KJV)** when we:

- refuse to acknowledge wrongdoing
- protect image instead of truth
- justify financial misuse as ministry
- silence our conviction for the sake of convenience

That is not merely making a mistake; it is sin. If you train your heart to live comfortably in deception, Scripture warns that the end of such a path is destruction, hell, judgement, and then the final destination is the lake of fire for eternity. Sin will always cost you more than you want to pay.

1) What happens to a soul when generosity becomes a tool?
2) What happens when offerings are received but never applied to the purpose for which they were given?
3) What happens when people are asked to sow into something *"God is doing,"* but leadership never intends to build what they declared?

These are not oversights, they are lies, violations of trust, and distortions of biblical stewardship. This is manipulation which is a form of witchcraft that so sadly takes place in the church. Can I get an *AMEN*?

Scripture is unmistakably clear, *"The LORD detests the use of dishonest scales, but he delights in accurate weights"* **(Proverbs 11:1 NLT)**. This is not about embarrassment, accusation, or revenge. It is about the truth in testimony, repentance, and the holiness God requires. This chapter is written not for the downfall of anyone; I would never want that. It is for the saving of many, healing of the body, integrity of the Gospel, and the fear of the Lord to be restored among His people.

How This Effects the Church

There is a particular kind of corruption that does not announce itself with scandal or spectacle but disguises itself as revelation, obedience, and spiritual urgency. It is the lie spoken not to protect the flock but to extract from it. When leaders distort truth to generate tithe, the altar becomes a marketplace, and the people become a means to an end rather than souls entrusted to care. This is not stewardship; it is spiritual manipulation wearing the language of faith.

Lies used to generate giving rarely sound like lies at first. They sound prophetic and urgent. They sound like God is about to withhold blessing unless obedience is proven through money. Fear is baptized as wisdom, pressure is reframed as faith, and questioning is labeled rebellion. The message becomes clear without ever being said directly, give or lose favor, sow or fall behind, and comply or be marked as faithless. This is dangerous because it teaches people to associate God's voice with anxiety rather than peace. Instead of learning discernment, believers learn survival. Instead of being discipled into generosity born from love, they are conditioned into fear-based compliance. Over time, the people stop asking whether something is true and begin asking only whether it is costly enough to keep them *"covered."* When money is extracted through deception the soul pays the price. Families give beyond their means because they believe withholding will bring judgment. Single mothers sow grocery money out of terror and elderly believers give retirement funds believing God demands it. When the promised breakthrough does not come, the blame is subtly placed back on the giver, not enough faith, sacrifice, or obedience. This practice fractures trust between the shepherd and the sheep. The pulpit ceases to be a place of refuge and becomes a lever of control for the benefit of the church structure. Scripture is no longer opened to reveal Christ but selectively wielded to reinforce authority and make a profit. The Word becomes a tool, not a truth, and once that line is crossed, the integrity of the entire ministry is compromised. Even more devastating is what this teaches people about God. He is no longer seen as a Father who gives freely but as a taskmaster who must be appeased. Grace is overshadowed by transaction. Love is replaced by leverage. The gospel is reduced to a system where blessing is bought; suffering is proof of personal failure.

A church that is willing to lie to the congregation to generate tithes may appear successful for a season, but it is hollow at its core. Growth becomes inflated, not healthy. Loyalty is enforced, not earned. When the structure eventually cracks, it is the people, not the leaders who bleed first. God does not need manipulation to fund His work, require lies and deception to accomplish His will, or anoint deception in His name. When lies are used to generate tithes, the issue is no longer financial, it is spiritual. The church is no longer being fed; it is being consumed. Where truth is sacrificed for revenue, judgment does not begin with the people; it begins at the pulpit.

Align yourself in the faithfulness of God not in the failures of men. Let Scripture not emotion, guide your understanding. Allow the Word of God, not opinion frame your discernment. Failure to keep silence should align you with what God Himself refuses to overlook. I share these accounts with trembling, not triumph because what happened did not just wound people; it revealed the deeper wounds within leadership, accountability, transparency, and the fear of the Lord.

The Addiction House That Never Was

In 2021, before we ever lived in Tennessee, Kasey and I were making the long drive from Indiana nearly every weekend, hungry for what God was doing and eager to be part of something bigger than ourselves. One Sunday morning, while we were still visitors, the wolf stood before the congregation with what seemed like a powerful God dream, an addiction recovery home. He painted the picture with passion, but it was woven in lies:

- where those battling addiction could find healing
- staffed with social workers and counselors
- where the broken could encounter Jesus and rebuild their lives

For us, this was not just another announcement. Kasey lit up. Everything in her knew, *"This is something I can help build."* We struggled in the area of addiction before the Lord saved us. So, we believed in the vision. When the wolf called the church to *"sow big,"* we did. We gave sacrificially, joyfully, and wholeheartedly. Once the offering was taken, the entire project went silent, not quieter, silent. Weeks passed, then months, not a single update. There was not a meeting or follow up, simply nothing. I eventually joined the staff and in

2022, I learned the truth. The church had purchased a decaying house on five acres up the road. It was an abandoned, broken property that sat empty for over a year. There were no:

- renovations
- planning
- preparations
- team
- outline timeline
- vision

When I asked a staff member what the plan was for the addiction home, they shrugged and said, *"There is no plan."* The house was eventually sold and to this day, I have no idea where the proceeds went. They never told the congregation the project had died or updated the people who gave; they simply moved on. Then came the moment that still sits heavy in my chest. One of our dear brothers, an elder in name only, passed away. Before he died, he confided in me more than once how frustrated he felt being labeled an *"elder"* yet never included in decisions, asked for input, or given a voice. He carried that burden to his grave. Shortly after his passing, the wolf stood before the church again and the same addiction house story returned. Only this time, he said it would be named after our friend who had just died. The people wept and the church rallied. Another *"special offering"* was taken. It was big, just like the first one. Would you classify this wolf as a professional con-artist? Just like before it was never brought to surface or mentioned again. Where are the funds? What did the wolf do with them both times? An offering was taken in the name of a deceased brother we loved deeply and then it vanished into the same silence as the first one. What the people believed they were giving toward never existed; not even as an idea or blueprint but a ploy to stir generosity. Once the offering buckets were full, the *"vision"* disappeared. What was presented as a mission from God was, in reality, nothing more than a money maker.

The School That Was Never a School

In 2022, our church made a big announcement that they were opening an elementary school. At least, that's what the congregation was told. In reality, what opened was not a school at all but a homeschool umbrella with almost no structure, oversight, or professional guidance. The wolf's sister-in-law, who had zero educational teaching background or administrative experience, simply decided one day that she wanted to run a school. She filled out the state paperwork and the church celebrated as though a fully functional Christian academy had been launched. Behind the scenes, the truth was much different. Two sheds were purchased, converted into *"classrooms,"* and set on the property. There was no standard curriculum or real academic accountability, and barely lawful record keeping; it was unorganized and made up as they went. Accountability, the very thing required by the state to ensure a child receives a legitimate education, never existed. The majority of the children were not receiving the instruction mandated by law and certainly not the education they deserved. The deeper you looked, the worse it became.

A young adult, a high school dropout, was given a diploma during a Sunday service in front of the entire congregation. She had never stepped foot in the school, not once. She had not completed any GED classes, assignments, or homeschool program. She did not have any of the credentials required for a diploma. The administrator wanted to give her parents *"the gift"* of seeing their daughter graduate since they never experienced that moment before. It was not a graduation but a performance built on a lie. The same thing happened with more than one child. Many children had not been doing schoolwork as they should have been doing. Yet diplomas were created for them, as if one could simply be printed into existence. I will never forget the words one administrator told me, *"A diploma is just a piece of paper. These children need this piece of paper, and I'm not going to ruin their life because parents did not make them do school."* That single statement summed up the entire culture, convenience over accountability, image over integrity, and appearance over truth. While this alone was a major ethical breach, it was not the end of it.

The Playground That Never Existed

Not long afterwards, the wolf took the pulpit again, but this time it was about fundraising for the school. He told the congregation we were adding on to the campus. We needed a security fence for a state-of-the-art playground. The wolf said we had blueprints and cost breakdowns. He said everything was ready except *the funds*. It stirred excitement and generosity. Parents, grandparents, and church members gave. People wanted their children and the church's children to have a safe place to learn and play. The truth that no one in the congregation knew was, no blueprints, plans, cost analysis, or any intention of building anything ever existed.

The children who were already missing the foundation of a sound education were now being used to fuel yet another emotional offering, another *"vision"* that evaporated the moment the buckets were collected. It was another promise spoken boldly from the pulpit, backed by nothing but the willingness of generous people to believe it. Just like everything else, the whole idea disappeared into silence as soon as the offering was over.

A Ministry Without Substance

After the elementary school had already revealed cracks beneath its surface, another, even more ambitious promise came from the pulpit, a full adult School of Ministry. It was not a Bible study or small discipleship group, but a full-blown ministry training institution where men and women would be equipped, trained, and eventually ordained for pastoral leadership. The wolf spoke of it as if it were already built. He told people to begin preparing their schedules and families to pray about relocating. The wolf described an atmosphere of learning, structure, mentorship, and theological development. It sounded impressive and sacred. People believed him but behind the scenes, the story was very different. There were conversations in staff meetings, yes, but they were the kind of conversations people have about dreams, not the kind of conversations people have about plans. There was no:

- curriculum
- academic framework
- accreditation process
- timeline
- preparation
- qualified educators

The wolf did not intend to lead the school himself. Instead, he assigned the responsibility to a staff member named Allen, a man who had no background in higher education and no experience creating a school of any kind. He was expected to somehow build an entire ministry college from scratch, as though it were as simple as choosing a paint color for a classroom. Now let us address the teachers. The wolf planned for staff

115

members, none of whom had teaching degrees, ministry training credentials, or collegiate experience, to serve as professors. These were wonderful people, but they were not qualified to teach biblical studies, theology, homiletics, counseling, or pastoral leadership at a collegiate level. Yet the wolf publicly claimed this would be a place where future pastors would be trained, tested, equipped, and even *ordained* into ministry. He was promising to raise, shape, and send out ministers into the world through a program that had no structure, oversight, or substance. People did not know this. They trusted what they heard from the pulpit. Families uprooted their lives, students moved across the country, and people saved money, set aside time, and prepared to enroll. They believed they were stepping into a place of spiritual development and pastoral preparation, a school that would shape their calling; it evaporated as well.

By late 2023, there were still no materials. By 2024, not a single class had been built. By 2025, the idea was never mentioned again. It was another promise spoken boldly and passionately, an announcement crafted to stir excitement and engagement, and a vision designed to attract attention, giving, and movement. Like the addiction house, playground, security fence, and elementary school, it disappeared into silence the moment the offering buckets were full; the emotional high had passed. Those who sacrificed the most, moved states, rearranged their lives, and believed they were answering a call, were left holding onto a dream that was never real.

Misrepresented Altar

There are moments in ministry that begin with such purity, expectation, and unmistakable hunger for God, that they mark you forever. One of those moments came on a Sunday morning when the wolf stood before the congregation and announced that we were going to build an altar. This was an altar where the very steps would carry the names of the people our church was believing for including:

- family members
- prodigals
- unsaved loved ones
- broken homes
- marriages hanging by threads
- children lost in addiction

It was a holy idea, one that stirred hope in the hearts of thousands. Names began pouring in from across America, even across the world. People who had never stepped foot in our church sent the names of sons, daughters, spouses, brothers, and sisters asking us to stand in the gap with them. What started as a simple idea became a flood of intercession.

Kasey and I, and to be fair the false prophetess along with some staff members spent *countless hours* writing each name, one by one, onto the steps of that altar. We took it seriously. Every name mattered. We prayed and wept as we wrote. Those steps became sacred to us, not because of the structure itself but because each name represented a soul someone loved enough to submit before the Lord. When we moved into the new building, the wolf proclaimed live on a Sunday morning that we would take the original altar from the old campus and create a memorial wall, an altar wall built with the very steps covered in the names of people we were committed to praying for. The congregation rejoiced at the thought. It was a beautiful vision, one that honored both the heart of intercession and the people who entrusted their loved ones to our prayers. Truthfully, we never gathered as a leadership group to pray cooperatively over those names, not one time. The only time the staff body prayed over those names were during live streamed services, when the cameras were rolling. Remember Saturday night prayer service? While congregants knelt at that altar crying out for their families and pleading for the names written there, loud music and laughter from staff parties echoed from the wolf's house. Prayer and weeping were interrupted in the sanctuary from shouting and celebration next door. Intercession met indifference and the spiritual weight of what those steps represented was never carried by the people entrusted to lead. That was never our heart. Kasey and I showed up. We prayed, interceded, and labored in love over those names because we believed every single one of them mattered to God. The collective leadership, the ones who cast the vision, called the church to bring names, and told the world these steps were sacred, never held a single private prayer gathering to honor the commitment they publicly made. An altar wall and intercession were promised. What the people received instead was neglect wrapped in emotion, a holy moment turned into a forgotten structure left to decay under the open sky. In that neglect, something in our hearts grieved, not just for the altar but for the people who trusted us to carry their names with reverence, believed we were standing with them, and families who thought their loved ones were being lifted before the Lord. The wall the wolf promised was never built. As of the end of 2025, that altar still sits at the old campus, exposed to the outside elements rotting away. The names of real people, stories, and souls were left weathered and forgotten.

Promises that Broke the Heart

There are moments in ministry that leave a mark so deep it reshapes the way you see God, people, and yourself. As I look back on the years we have walked through, the addiction house that never was, diplomas that were handed out without merit, elementary school built on sheds instead of structure, playground and fencing that were never planned, school of ministry that never moved beyond a microphone, and the altar, I find myself wrestling with a mixture of:

- grief because the people of God deserved truth
- conviction because I stayed silent longer than I should have
- gratitude because the Lord, in His mercy, refused to let the darkness have the final say

Scripture says, *"The integrity of the upright guides them, but the crookedness of the treacherous destroys them"* **(Proverbs 11:3 ESV)**. When integrity is abandoned, whether in small decisions or in public promises, the path eventually caves in beneath those who walk in it. What has come to light in these years is not merely poor planning or broken administration. It is the slow erosion of integrity, quiet death of truth, and spiritual decay that happens when image becomes more important than truth. I have had to ask myself difficult questions I did not want to face:

- How many times did I see red flags and looked away because it was easier?
- How many times did I sense the Holy Spirit nudging me to speak, and I stayed silent?
- How many moments did I choose peace in the room over peace with God?

These questions hurt, but they have healed me more than the answers ever did. The Lord began to remind me of His Word, His unchanging, immovable, and piercing Word: *"...be sure your sin will find you out"* **(Numbers 32:23 NKJV)**. *"For nothing is hidden that will not be revealed..."* **(Luke 8:17 WEB)**. *"Woe to the shepherds*

who destroy and scatter the sheep of My pasture!"
(*Jeremiah 23:1* NKJV). Every verse felt like God was
placing a hand on my shoulder saying, *"I saw what you
saw, and I saw what you did not."* Yet, He did not
speak to bring condemnation. He spoke to bring clarity,
call me out of complicity, and remind me that His
Kingdom is built on truth, not theatrics. In the quiet
moments with the Lord, I have realized something else,
we were not just witnessing the collapse of projects but
also the collapse of character. If we had chosen to stay
would our character have become like the wolf and
false prophetess? I am thankful for God's mercy. He
has been faithful while correcting, cleansing, calling us
deeper, restoring our fear of Him, and realigning our
hearts with His. David prayed, *"Search me, O God, and
know my heart: try me, and know my thoughts: And see
if there be any wicked way in me, and lead me in the
way everlasting"* **(*Psalm 139:23–24* KJV)**. God is still
writing the story. What was built on lies will fall and
that which was built on truth will stand. God sees
everyone that has been hurt, confused, misled, or
wounded.

Healing Begins
Scripture does not tell you to pretend harm was holy.
Jesus rebuked leaders who *"tie up heavy burdens"* and
lay them on people without lifting a finger to help
(*Matthew 23:4* KJV). When giving is pressured through
fear, threats, or false promises, you are not being
discipled; you are being controlled. Call it what it is. If
it produced fear, confusion, and compulsion, that fruit
is evil and corrupt **(*Matthew 7:15–20* KJV)**. Truth is not
afraid of the light **(*John 3:20–21* KJV)**.
"For God is not the author of confusion" **(*1 Corinthians
14:33* NKJV)**. If the *"prompting"* you feel is dominated by
dread, *"give or else, sow or else, you will be cursed if*
120

you do not," that is not the Shepherd's voice; it is the wolf speaking: *"My sheep hear My voice… and they follow Me"* **(John 10:27 NKJV).** The Scripture teaches we cannot buy God with money or any other substance. He is not for sale: *"Every man according as he purposeth in his heart, so let him give; not grudgingly, or of necessity: for God loveth a cheerful giver"* **(2 Corinthians 9:7 KJV).** *"Not of necessity"* means God does not want anyone to give because they feel forced or pressured. No one gets to threaten your destiny to access your wallet. The purpose in your heart means God honors conscience, prayer, and wisdom. This is why healing includes relearning so you can say, *"No, not right now, I will pray about it"* without fear of punishment from God.

Manipulative systems often attach curses to disobedience to keep you compliant. Jesus became a curse for us **(Galatians 3:13 KJV).** If you have been living with dread or waiting for disaster because you left or stopped giving, renounce that fear in prayer. You are not under man-made spiritual threats; you are under the blood of Jesus. *"Christ hath redeemed us"* is not poetic, it is legal language of deliverance. Your future is not governed by a pulpit. Your life is governed by the Word of God.

Chapter 8
Deliverance Ministry

Jesus and the Heart of Freedom

Deliverance is not a trend, modern movement, charismatic novelty, and certainly not a special assignment for a select few. It is woven into the very fabric of our Savior's earthly ministry. It reveals the heart of God toward the broken, oppressed, and all who sit in the shadows of bondage. In Scripture, deliverance is never presented as a side ministry; it is part of the Gospel itself. When Jesus stood in the synagogue of Nazareth and read from the prophet Isaiah, He made His mission unmistakably clear: *"The Spirit of the Lord is upon me, because he hath anointed me to preach the gospel to the poor; he hath sent me to heal the broken-hearted, to preach deliverance to the captives, and recovering of sight to the blind, to set at liberty them that are bruised"* **(Luke 4:18 KJV)**. Freedom was not an extra bonus; it was the very heartbeat of Jesus' ministry.

In the synagogue when a man with an unclean spirit cried out **(Mark 1:21–27 KJV)**, Jesus did not panic or perform, He simply spoke: *"Hold thy peace, and come out of him."* There was no theatrics or chaos, just divine authority. The people marveled, not because of noise but because His authority was genuine.

We then see Him cross an entire sea through a storm for the sake of one tormented soul in the country of the Gadarenes **(Mark 5:1–20 KJV)**. Everyone else had abandoned this man, but Jesus traveled miles for his freedom. The heart of biblical deliverance is personal, intentional, and deeply compassionate. The man did not walk away confused or broken. He sat *"clothed, and in his right mind."* Jesus also delivered children **(Mark 9:17– 27 KJV)**. A father cried out for his son who had suffered since childhood and Jesus spoke tenderly, took the boy by the hand, and lifted him up. Deliverance was never a performance; it was restoration.

In other moments, Jesus delivered people privately away from the crowds proving again that freedom was never meant to be a spectacle but an act of love, dignity, and holy compassion. He cared not for manifestations but for souls. This is the same Jesus who declared, *"If the Son therefore shall make you free, ye shall be free indeed"* **(John 8:36 KJV)**. Deliverance and freedom come through His authority and when demonstrated, you see His love for mankind. Jesus taught us how to handle deliverance; He commissioned His Church to continue it: *"...in my name shall they cast out devils..."* **(Mark 16:17 KJV)**. In **Acts 16**, Paul commanded a spirit of divination to depart with a single sentence. He did not put on theatrical deliverance shows. The book of Acts is a book of deliverance, healing, and signs and wonders, not for entertainment but to reveal the living Christ in the midst of His people. The purpose of deliverance is to set the captives free.

Witnessed

Before we speak of the painful things that happened, we must first honor the truth we witnessed through the power of God that move beautifully in our church. We saw the Holy Spirit do works that only the one true God can do and these miracles still take my breath away whenever I recall them. I prayed with a man whose cancer vanished after the Lord touched his body and watched a woman who was blind walk out seeing again. I saw marriages restored, addictions broken, depression lifted, fear departed, and people who walked in torment left clothed in peace. Young people fell in love with Jesus again, families were healed, and hearts once hardened become soft in His presence. We witnessed people walk in broken and left whole, bound and left free, and lost and were found. I am *NOT* against deliverance done God's way; it is beautiful and life changing.

When deliverance becomes a theatrical show and admission is required at some events, the Holy Spirit is deeply grieved. We saw methods and practices that wounded people and approaches that created confusion, fear, and emotional trauma. We also saw environments that resulted in a mass exodus of sincere believers, not because deliverance was wrong, but because the techniques and theatrics that developed over time no longer reflected the Jesus we see in the Scriptures: *"If the Son therefore shall make you free, ye shall be free indeed"* (*John 8:36* KJV).

This is the story of how we lost our way. The Father, in His mercy, began opening our eyes one moment at a time. As the months passed, something in the atmosphere of our ministry began to shift. Slowly at first, like a single thread loosening at the corner of a garment, began an unraveling move of God that gradually became something unrecognizable to us. I say this not as an outsider but as someone who stood in the rooms, prayed with the people, held trembling hands, and wiped their tears. Somewhere along the way deliverance drifted from the heart of Jesus and became a tool to draw crowds. It became a spectacle designed to keep people and money coming in as an unspoken strategy that fueled the *Big Corrupt Church*. The pureness of deliverance became public, system led, and all about numbers. I do not write this as a critic but a witness.

124

These were things I saw and carried home in my chest at night that left me grieving, conflicted, and wrestling with the difference between the God I knew and the methods unfolding before my eyes. The beauty of deliverance did not vanish all at once; it eroded slowly, moment by moment, compromise by compromise, and red flag by red flag, until the ministry I once cherished no longer resembled the Jesus who first called me. The following is my raw, unfiltered, and sincere testimony. It was an account of the moments, teachings, practices, and the experiences that revealed just how far we had drifted and how desperately we needed His correction. In 2022, when our church first stepped into deliverance ministry, everything felt raw, holy, and deeply personal. We were not seeking platforms, moments, chasing spectacles, or trying to build a name; we were just simply trying to meet people where they were. I remember those early days vividly. We spent hours in small rooms with hurting souls, praying, listening, waiting, discerning, and doing everything we knew to do to be vessels the Lord could use. We would arrive at the church around eight in the morning and not leave until nearly midnight. It was beautiful and exhausting, holy and heavy. Every part of our lives became consumed with casting out devils. At the time, we truly believed we were carrying the heart of Jesus into every moment.

However, somewhere along the way something shifted. As crowds grew and needs multiplied the work began to feel impossible. People lined up outside our building with desperation in their eyes. There were not enough hours in the day or enough hands to minister to the tidal wave of people seeking freedom. Out of that pressure an idea surfaced. The wolf suggested, *"What if we did a mass deliverance? One moment, one prayer, and one call for the whole room. It would save time, energy, and help the deliverance ministers catch their breath."*

At first, it sounded strategic, almost efficient. A way to serve more people in less time. Scripture whispered something different. When Jesus cast out demons, He did not do it through blanket declarations and shout into crowds hoping the right person would receive the miracle. He met people individually by name, need, and story. He saw the one woman bowed down for eighteen years and called her forward **(Luke 13:11–13 KJV)**. He approached the one boy tormented from childhood and spoke directly to that unclean spirit **(Mark 9:17–27 KJV)**. Another time, Jesus crossed an entire sea to free one man dwelling among the tombs **(Mark 5:1–20 KJV)**. Deliverance was never an act of efficiency for Jesus; it was an act of encountering.

When mass deliverance began, I expected unity and holy alignment with heaven. However, chaos erupted almost instantly. Children were being restrained as their bodies thrashed around. People were being held down, not gently but forcefully. Some became aggressive, swinging at whoever was closest while others bolted out of the building, sprinting through the parking lot in terror. They stole cars, wrecked them, screamed, tore up chairs, vomited, and even bled from their noses. What happened in that sanctuary bore no resemblance to the orderly authority of Christ. The room felt less like holy ground and more like a spiritual emergency room with no physicians. As I stood there taking in the confusion, one Scripture rose louder than the noise around me: *"For God is not the author of confusion, but of peace…"* **(1 Corinthians 14:33 KJV)**. The Jesus I knew did not create chaos, He calmed it. In that moment, a painful truth settled over me; we had drifted from the heart of the Father all in the name of convenience and efficiency. Deliverance started with compassion, personal one-on-one, and moved by love. However, when mass deliverance began the crowd was uncontrollable. The mass declarations were just simply overwhelmed by numbers, no order or peaceful conduct. Jesus never sacrificed the individual for the convenience of the moment. Every deliverance, healing, and miracle He performed was saturated with tenderness, intentionality, and personal connection. Mass deliverance took us far from that. As I stood watching the frenzy unfold, grief rose in my spirit, not only because of what I saw but because I knew deep in my soul that the Father never intended ministry to look like this. The chaos before me did not reveal the power of God; it revealed how far we had drifted from His holiness. This was a red flag moment that rose in my heart where something inside me began to break and awaken. I realized that mass deliverance without the heart of Jesus can look like deliverance but be far from it. I am guilty of mistaking momentum for anointing, making decisions through exhaustion, letting the crowd set the pace instead of the Holy Spirit, and accepting methods simply because they were called normal even though it went against Scripture. The Lord began to teach me gently and slowly through Scripture what true deliverance really looks like.

What We Forgot

When I finally slowed down long enough to breathe and opened my Bible again, not as a deliverance minister or staff member but simply as a disciple, I began to see something I had missed far too long. Scripture always presents deliverance as personal, intentional, and inseparable from discipleship. The ministry of Jesus was unquestionably powerful, yet it was also unmistakably specific. It was never rushed, chaotic, or a blanket command thrown across a room

127

hoping to land on the right person. Jesus did not treat people as a crowd to conquer; He ministered to each individual. It is the intimate work of a Shepherd tending His sheep, a Father healing His child, and a Savior restoring the brokenhearted. Deliverance is not about a performance; it is always about setting the captive free. To walk in freedom, you must have discipleship. Jesus did not simply cast out spirits and walk away, He said, *"Follow Me."* Every deliverance was an invitation into relationship and holiness.

Discipleship Guards Deliverance
When deliverance and discipleship are separated, it begins to drift from what scripture taught us demonstrated through Jesus. In the beginning of our ministry, we did not know how to tell the difference between the Spirit of God and human emotion. For example, when people cried and screamed loudly, we assumed it meant breakthrough or demons manifesting. As the crowd surged, we assumed God was sweeping through the room but did not know it was emotionalism. Emotionalism does not always occur with shouting; it can be subtle or an adrenaline rush. It is like a domino effect. Scripture paints a very different picture. Elijah did not find God in the wind, the earthquake, or the fire; but in *"a still small voice"* **(1 Kings 19:11–12 KJV)**. The fruit of the Spirit produces self-control, not out of control **(Galatians 5:22–23 KJV)**. True deliverance is powerful, supernatural, intense, and real. It is never disorderly, unsafe, abusive, or chaotic. God is merciful in His correction. He does not shame from a distance; He whispers in the middle of the mess.

Unbiblical Consequences

There was a time in ministry when we were all desperately trying to understand deliverance, but instead of learning through wisdom or Scripture, we absorbed it through a distorted lens of fear, pressure, and the absolute certainty of leaders who believed their understanding was 100% correct. We were taught things with a boldness that made us feel they could not possibly be wrong. Looking back, that confidence should have been a red flag. One teaching repeated constantly was that medication could block healing or deliverance. We were told that pharmaceutical treatments were the spirit of *"Pharmakeia"* which can create a spiritual barrier and if you wanted to be healed, you needed to stop taking your medication. I remember sitting through those teachings, feeling my stomach twist every time it was said. Something felt off, but we trusted the wolf's leaders. We believed they were speaking from revelation. They spoke with such authority that questioning them felt like doubting what the Lord had shown them. I didn't know enough about deliverance ministry at the time to challenge their teaching.

Then came the day everything changed. A staff member conducted a deliverance session with a young man who had diabetes. I was not in the room so I don't know what words were exchanged, but I remember hearing afterwards that something significant had happened. I learned that after this meeting he had apparently stopped taking his insulin. Whether he was told directly, interpreted the teaching as a command, or was afraid of being *"blocked"* from healing was unsure; we may never know why he stopped his insulin. I do know this; he trusted the teaching enough to stop the very medication that kept him alive. Not long after his deliverance session, we got the news that he had died.

We found out over a text message. The shock hit like a physical blow. I remember the way the atmosphere around me changed, the stunned silence and sick heaviness that settled over everything. I remember sitting with the sinking realization that something irreversible had happened and that the beliefs we were being fed were not harmless but dangerous. Leadership should never put that yoke upon people. Not all medication can simply be stopped without serious consequences to the human body. In the days that followed, there were no conversations, reflections, or accountability. There was just a quiet tension hanging over the building like a fog that no one wanted to acknowledge. We didn't talk about or work through it, absolutely nothing. One day, out of nowhere, we received a voice memo from the false prophetess. Her tone was serious, almost clinical. She simply said something along the lines of *"from that point forward, we were no longer permitted to tell people that medication prevents healing or deliverance."* There were no apologies, explanations, or ownership of the lies we were taught. It was just a quick reversal of something that had been preached from the pulpit with absolute conviction, now dismissed by a voice memo and it better quietly disappear. As for me, that moment was searing because a life had been lost in the gap between misplaced theology and medical reality. The ignorance of that season was not innocent, harmless, or a small misinterpretation of Scripture; it was plain arrogance wearing the costume of faith and it cost a young man everything. What a man preaches from the platform in a church holds consequences for his followers. We are accountable to the Lord and His people for our teachings, even if we unintentionally mislead people from a place of good intention. That tragedy lodged itself deep inside me. It made me realize

130

that spiritual authority, when unexamined and unrestrained, can become lethal. It taught me that faith without wisdom is not faith at all; it is presumption and presumption can destroy people. It was one of the first moments I realized something profoundly painful, when a ministry becomes more committed to being right than being responsible, people get hurt. Sometimes, they don't survive.

Abuse Covered Up

There are moments in ministry you walk away changed, not because of what you taught or how God moved but because of what your spirit was forced to hold. In the first part of our ministry, I had one of the most disturbing experiences of my life which began quietly during a deliverance session. This deliverance led to a conversation I never expected to have. A young person connected to leadership approached me shaking in a way I had never seen them before. Their voice was barely above a whisper, eyes darting as if the walls themselves were listening. They told me something that made the air feel thick, something that made my heart pound inside my chest. They confessed to me in their own words and trembling voice, that they had sexually abused their sibling in the past. I am not sure if what was spoken was true because their eyes were darting back and forth. I questioned if this person was under the influence of a substance. It felt like the room froze. I remember blinking slowly because everything inside me felt like it had suddenly detached from reality. I did not know what to say or if even to breathe.

I was placed in possession of information involving a serious allegation for which I had no formal training, legal guidance, or institutional protection. In good faith and while under significant distress, I immediately brought this information to the appropriate leadership

131

and parent involved and was assured by all adult parties involved that appropriate protocols would be followed. During this meeting, I was explicitly instructed that the matter was to remain confidential and that it was not to be disclosed to any outside parties. I was directly warned that I was not to contact the Department of Child Services (DCS), law enforcement, or any other governmental, regulatory, or enforcement agency. I was further told that if I reported the matter, sought assistance, or disclosed the information through any external or reporting channels, my employment would be terminated immediately because they were taking care of the matter. These statements were communicated by individuals in positions of authority and were understood by me as a direct threat of retaliation intended to prevent reporting by me. The instruction to remain silent combined with the explicit warning of job loss, created a coercive environment that left me fearful of the consequences of acting in accordance with my beliefs. I felt like I was drowning in a secret that did not belong to me but had somehow been fastened to my soul. I am unaware if either of the children received professional counseling or any safeguards were put in place. Life moved on as if nothing had been said and I noticed that they were still left alone together at times. Watching that with the confession echoing in my mind was like swallowing glass.

Our office did not have running water, so whenever we needed to use the restroom, we had to walk to the head office located in the main lobby of the building. The lobby was on the first floor and as you entered, the wolf's office loft was immediately visible within that space. The restrooms were also located in the main lobby, making it impossible to pass through without seeing or hearing what was happening there. One day I walked to the main lobby with my spouse to use the restroom. The moment we entered, we could both see and hear that something was wrong. Inside the wolf's office, a ministry-led *"deliverance session"* was already underway. Two in-house security officers were physically restraining a child whose body was thrashing violently. The scene was open, visible from the main lobby and impossible to avoid. We continued toward the restroom but even there the sounds followed us; there were raised voices, loud prayers, and cries that were unmistakably coming from a place of deep distress. Nothing about what I was hearing sounded like healing. It felt like a spiritual emergency being addressed with tools that were never meant to handle trauma. The cries I heard were not cries of freedom or release; they were the cries of someone carrying a wound far deeper than anyone in that room seemed equipped to understand. There were no licensed counselors present, trauma-informed care, sense of safety, or grounding. There were only loud prayers, raised voices, and the assumption that what this child needed was deliverance, not comfort, protection, or a therapist. I remember standing there with my hands trembling, trying to reconcile what I was witnessing with the language being used to justify it. The atmosphere felt frantic, electric, and chaotic. A child's anguish had become something observed, managed, and explained away in spiritual terms and something in me knew this was terribly wrong. Hearing what was taking place, those words felt painfully hollow. By the time we left the restroom, my spouse and I did not need to discuss it. We walked out of the building, got into our truck, and went home, carrying with us the weight of what we had seen and heard. What stayed with me then and still stays with me now, was the clarity of a single thought, that was not deliverance; it was desperation.

133

The helplessness I felt watching a wounded child be treated as if the problem was spiritual misalignment instead of a deep, unseen trauma was horrifying. The shock of it did not fade, it settled.

I walked into ministry believing I was stepping into a family of believers. However, I walked out learning that sometimes the places we expect to be the safest can become the very places where wounds are covered instead of healed, confessions are buried instead of addressed, and the vulnerable are handled with methods that make them break even more. Sometimes, they become the very reason a person finally says, *"I can't stay silent anymore."*

There are still nights when I sit with the memory of that season and my chest tightens the same way it did back then. I replay the looks, moments, and sounds but most of all the silence. The silence is what lingers. I wish I could say I stood up immediately and knew exactly what to do, but the truth is I did not. I was young, had a family, and a responsibility to provide for them. I was hopeful, trusting, and eager to serve God but completely unprepared for the weight people began placing in my hands. Looking back now, I can see how far we had drifted from the heart of the Father. We were trained to be loyal, silent, and conditioned to believe that unity meant agreement, even when everything inside us screamed that something was wrong. I did not recognize it then, but now I see it clearly; obedience to man had slowly replaced obedience to God. I grieved that I:

- didn't speak up sooner
- didn't question what clearly violated wisdom, safety, and Scripture
- carried someone else's trauma
- stayed silent when a child needed an advocate, not a ministry team

I once believed silence, obedience, and peace meant compliance. Now I know silence can imprison, obedience belongs to the Shepherd, and true wisdom is first pure, then peaceable *"But the wisdom that is from above is first pure, then peaceable…"* **(James 3:17 KJV)**. Peace without purity isn't peace, it's compromise. When I read the Gospels now, I see a Jesus who never ignored the vulnerable, turned someone's pain into a spectacle, and hid truth to protect an image. He plainly said, *"…Inasmuch as ye have done it unto one of the least of these… ye have done it unto me"* **(Matthew 25:40 KJV)**. I cannot help but ask myself did we:

- protect the least of these
- protect the ministry
- comfort the hurting
- manage the moment
- follow Jesus
- follow culture, charisma, pressure, and fear

These are the questions that keep me awake, not from bitterness but from the lack of accountability. I cannot undo what I witnessed, the silence I was forced into, choices leadership made, or the possible harm that child endured. I cannot change the past, but I can refuse silence now, tell the truth, repent where I participated in harmful systems, and place my failures at the foot of the cross. I am thankful for the mercy of a God who restores and heals. I can let regret instruct me rather than imprison me and I can warn others because what happened was not ministry, Jesus, or Love. It was confusion and *"For God is not the author of confusion…"* **(1 Corinthians 14:33 KJV)**.

Counterfeit Deliverance

There is a line in deliverance ministry that most people never realize exists, between the true supernatural power of God and its counterfeit, authority of Jesus and the theatrics of human imagination, and biblical deliverance and something frighteningly close to witchcraft. The truth is painfully simple; you do not have to be a witch to practice witchcraft; you only have to trust an experience more than the Word of God. In our church, that line began to blur long before anyone noticed.

The false prophetess played a central role in deliverance, yet many of the methods she taught us did not come from Scripture. They came from visions, impressions, so called spiritual *"downloads,"* and techniques that sounded supernatural but had no biblical foundation whatsoever. At first, we didn't question any of it. We were earnest, hungry, wanted to help people, and assumed that anything producing a reaction must have been spiritual. Over time, what we witnessed drifted far beyond anything Scripture describes.

We watched her step up to people and claim she was pulling *"jewels"* out of their stomachs, as though invisible treasures were lodged inside their bodies. We witnessed her carry-on long arguments with what she called *"ancient demons,"* speaking to them for extended periods as if they were partners in conversation rather than liars bound by darkness. She also reached into the air and *"ripped out"* invisible tentacles, arrows, snakes, nests, eggs, webs, and other supposedly spiritual objects that no one else could see. She told desperate people that they could not be delivered because they had not forgiven quickly enough, using condemnation as her tool rather than compassion. We saw deliverance devolve into pure emotionalism such as yelling, striking people on their backs, forcing reactions, and demanding manifestations simply to prove that something, anything, was happening. The false prophetess talked directly to demons, asking them what else was *"inside"* the person, treating their words as if they held truth rather than deception. She and others began guessing at spirits, calling out random names until one triggered a reaction, turning deliverance into a kind of spiritual lottery where accuracy mattered less than drama. This was truly a demon circus. People responded through crying, screaming, convulsing, and vomiting. The room erupted with dramatic manifestations that looked spiritual to the untrained eye, but reactions alone do not confirm truth. What we were witnessing was not the fruit of biblical deliverance; it was the fruit of confusion, manipulation, and emotional pressure disguised as ministry.

Nonbiblical

Not once did Jesus dig spiritual objects out of people's bodies, nor did He pull demonic jewels, eggs, or tentacles from anyone. He did not:

- interrogate demons in long drawn-out conversations
- strike people in an attempt to force a manifestation
- guess at names of random spirits until one reacted
- blame a lack of forgiveness for someone's inability to be delivered
- stir chaos to demonstrate His power
- allow demons to direct or define the ministry taking place

Scripture tells us clearly that Jesus cast out demons *"with his word"* (**Matthew 8:16 KJV**), not with theatrics, rituals, or guesswork but simply with a word. He did not wrestle with demons, argue with them, gather

137

information from spirits that cannot tell the truth, or depend on emotionalism or spectacle to prove His authority. Jesus operated from the power of His identity and the certainty of His authority, not from adrenaline or performance. When deliverance turns into scraping invisible objects off bodies, summoning demons to talk, demanding manifestations, or relying on imagination instead of Scripture, it stops being deliverance and starts resembling the occult. Witchcraft is not limited to spells or potions. Witchcraft is any spiritual practice divorced from the Word of God and driven by human imagination, manipulation, fear, or control. The Bible could not draw the contrast any clearer. *Witchcraft* chases hidden knowledge, but *deliverance* breaks chains and sets captives free. *It* manipulates unseen realms, but *deliverance* bows to the absolute authority of Jesus Christ. *Witchcraft* thrives on dramatic rituals, yet *true deliverance* stands firmly on the Word and the Spirit. *It* converses with demons, while Jesus silenced them with a single command. *Witchcraft* demands emotional reaction to feel powerful, but the Holy Spirit produces real peace.

Even when intentions are good, deliverance becomes dangerous the moment it drifts from the Bible. The most frightening part is it begins to mirror the very thing it claims to cast out. True deliverance never elevates the experience; it elevates Christ. It never glorifies the battle; it glorifies the One who already won. Genuine deliverance does not traumatize but restores, heals, and brings the soul back to life. If a deliverance moment does anything other than lead someone closer to Jesus, it is not deliverance but distraction, distortion, and spiritual danger wrapped in spiritual language.

True Freedom

There is something very tender I want to speak into with the heart of a pastor. The deliverances many of you experienced when hands were laid on you, prayed over you, or when the false prophetess ministered to you felt intense, emotional, and deeply personal. I want you to receive this with complete peace in your spirit; if you experienced freedom, that freedom was real, and it came from the Lord, not from any person. Please realize God delivers, heals, and breaks chains. People can encourage us, pray with us, and walk beside us, but no human being alone, no matter their gifting or sincerity has the power to set a captive free. Only the Spirit of the Living God can do that. Let your heart rest and your mind be at peace.

Deliverance Becomes Performance

There came a point in our journey when deliverance stopped feeling like ministry and started resembling a stage production. Some of the clearest red flags did not come from within our own church but from the guest speakers who were invited by the wolf and false prophetess to *"train"* us. On the surface, their presence seemed exciting. These were men and women with national platforms, known for what they called powerful deliverance ministries. They arrived with confidence, charisma, and an air of spiritual expertise. What unfolded on our stage bore little resemblance to the Jesus I knew from Scripture. Instead of shepherds tending to the hurting, we watched performers stepping into roles that felt dramatic, exaggerated, and disturbingly disconnected from the heart of Christ. One guest minister in particular treated deliverance as theater. They would call someone onto the stage and speak with them for barely thirty seconds. Then it would suddenly shift into a dramatic stance that looked more like a supernatural pose than a moment of prayer. There was no Scripture, command, or compassion, just a demonic theatrical show. Sadly, the only thing missing was the popcorn. Every time the performer on the stage would react violently, their back would arch, limbs would flail, and screams would pierce the sanctuary. The minister ignored the individuals need and treated him/her like a prop. I will never forget one woman who walked off the stage afterward; she was shaken, confused, and spiritually disoriented. Nothing in her face said freedom. Nothing in her posture said peace. She walked off the stage even more broken. Yet the crowd applauded, simply because the spectacle looked impressive.

Another guest minister turned deliverance into combat entertainment. Every moment resembled a supernatural boxing match. They shouted at demons with dramatic flair, jerking their body backward every time the person manifesting said something. The minister was acting as though invisible blows were landing. It became a choreographed sequence, the demon shouts, the minister staggers, the crowd gasps, and the minister recovers triumphantly. The entire moment looked like a scene from a movie, not the ministry of Jesus. People were not being helped; they were being entertained. This was almost like a box office theater. What confused me most was how little any of this resembled Scripture. Not once in the Gospels do we see Jesus inviting people onto a platform to demonstrate deliverance. He never turned someone's suffering into a teaching illustration, nor did He pose dramatically to stir reactions. Jesus never mimicked combat with demons or exaggerated His movements to impress the crowd. His deliverance ministry was marked by authority, compassion, clarity, and privacy. We were seeing the exact opposite. Demons were given platforms and microphones. Jesus said, *"Wherefore by their fruits ye shall know them"* **(Matthew 7:20 KJV)**. The fruit on those nights was not freedom; it was fear, chaos, and hunger for the next dramatic moment. That season of deliverance mixed with hidden abuse marked a turning point in my walk with God. It shattered assumptions I had carried about deliverance, healing, leadership, and spiritual authority. It forced me to ask questions I had been too afraid or conditioned to ask before. These were not questions of rebellion; they were questions born out of responsibility, compassion, and truth. I could bring them only to my Father in Heaven because questioning leadership was forbidden. That burden was heavy and it pressed into every part of my spirit. So, I returned to Scripture with new eyes. I wasn't searching for verses to defend what I had been taught; I was searching for Jesus. What I found surprised me. The Jesus of the Gospels never weaponized healing against the weak or demanded someone abandon wisdom to prove faith. Healing is not a test; it is a gift. Gifts are never earned by risking your life to prove loyalty.

The more I studied Christ, the more I saw how far certain teachings had drifted from His example. Scripture says, *"My people are destroyed for lack of knowledge..."* **(Hosea 4:6 KJV)**. For years I believed that referred only to head knowledge. Now I understand it also speaks to the lack of wise, humble, and discerning leadership. Jesus heals bodies through miracles that defy earthly limitation; heals hearts through the nearness of His presence, where brokenness dissolves in the warmth of His love. He heals minds through the unshakable truth of His Word and memories through the tender mercy that rewrites what pain once claimed.

Reflection

We assume that because a leader said it, God must have endorsed it. The Bible reminds us, *"Test all things; hold fast what is good"* (**1 Thessalonians 5:21** NKJV). You are biblically allowed to examine what you were taught, acknowledge when something was harmful, and unlearn what was spoken over you in fear or control. Jesus does not need you to pretend something spiritual was healthy when it was not. He is kind enough to walk into the places that still hurt and bring truth where lies once lived. The Holy Spirit is a Comforter, not a tormentor. He leads us into truth gently with clarity and peace.

Personal Reflection

Sometimes I have to sit before God and admit what I did not want to see. I believed things He never said, carried weights He never placed on me, and feared consequences He never threatened. So, I come to Him with truth, trembling, and the kind of humility that only comes after realizing I was wrong. *"Lord, teach me again. Teach me right. Teach me truth."* I confess that there were moments when I confused man's confidence with Your authority. I repeated things because they were taught loudly, not because they were taught biblically and trusted methods that promised power more than the gentle, faithful work of Your Spirit. Father allow me to walk in Your fear and not the fear of man. Help me to be the person You created me to be. Allow me to decrease and You to increase in my life every day. Thank you for Your grace and mercy.

Our Prayer for the Reader

May the Lord Jesus, the Shepherd of your soul, draw you close in this moment with a peacc that passes all understanding. Let His Word be the lamp to your feet and the light to your path, guiding you gently out of old pain and into fresh healing. May every place in you that has been wounded by people be restored by the hands of the One who will never fail you. Allow His voice to steady your spirit, silence your fear, and renew your hope. Let the Holy Spirit surround you with comfort, remind you of truth, and lead you step by step into wholeness. May the Father, who sees the deepest parts of your heart, cover you with His love, guard your mind with His peace, and keep you close to His presence all your days. Do not leave carrying the weight of what hurt you but carrying the healing of the One who holds you. In the name of Jesus, who restores, rebuilds, and renews. Amen.

Chapter 9
Prophetic Turns Poisonous

Red Flag: **Lies from the Pulpit**

Knowing the Difference

Prophecy is the message and act of speaking forth what
God reveals. It is not primarily about predicting the
future; it is about declaring God's will, word, or
warning: *"But he that prophesieth speaketh unto men to
edification, and exhortation, and comfort"* (**1 Corinthians
14:3 KJV**). Prophecy includes:
- declaring God's truth
- calling people to repentance
- warning, instruction, or encouragement
- sometimes revealing future events, but always
  in alignment with God's Word

Prophecy is something God gives; it is not a title.

Who is a Prophet?

A prophet is a person called and appointed by God to
consistently carry and steward prophetic revelation:
*"Surely the Lord GOD will do nothing, but he revealeth
his secret unto his servants the prophets"* (**Amos 3:7 KJV**).
A prophet:
- stands as a watchman
- speaks God's word with authority and
  accountability
- is often sent to confront kings, leaders, or
  nations
- bears responsibility for accuracy, obedience,
  and character

Not everyone who prophesies is a prophet.

What Profit is Not:

Profit with an *"i"* is a financial gain, not a spiritual
office: *"...supposing that gain is godliness: from such*

144

withdraw thyself" **(1 Timothy 6:5 KJV)**. Confusing *prophet with profit* is not just a spelling or a phonetic issue; it can become a spiritual one when ministry is driven by gain rather than obedience. ***Key biblical distinction:***

- Many may prophesy
- Few are called as prophets
- Prophecy serves the body
- Prophets serve God's purpose, often at personal cost *"...would God that all the LORD's people were prophets, and that the LORD would put his spirit upon them!"* **(Numbers 11:29 KJV)**.

Simple summary:

- Prophecy equals the message
- Prophet equals the messenger
- Profit equals money, not ministry

True prophecy always aligns with Scripture, glorifies God, and calls people back to holiness, not toward personal gain.

A Call for Discernment

Prophecy is a beautiful gift from God, given to individuals to hear and perceive in the spiritual realm. Like a radio, it receives signals, frequencies, or channels, but discernment is required to determine whether what is being received is truly from God. Not every voice, impression, or vision is of the Spirit of truth. Scripture instructs us to *"try the spirits by the Word of God"* to discern whether what we are hearing or seeing is truth or deception **(1 John 4:1 KJV)**.

When prophecy is not tested, it is easy to be misled. The same gift that can carry the weight of declaring God's judgment to nations is also meant to edify, exhort, and comfort the body of Christ **(1 Corinthians 14:3 KJV)**. Prophecy is not fortune-telling, chasing predictions, or spiritual performance. It is the heart of God spoken through the mouth of a surrendered vessel

145

carrying His truth, timing, tenderness, and works in love.

True prophecy is meant to build, not to bind. It strengthens faith, brings clarity, stirs repentance, and draws people closer to the Father. Above all, it reflects the Word of our Savior, full of grace and truth. Scripture also gives us strong and sobering counsel, not every voice that claims to speak for God is from Him. Jesus Himself warned us to *"beware of wolves in sheep's clothing."* There are people who wear the appearance of spirituality but lack the fruit of the Spirit. He did not tell us to judge their charisma, accuracy, or gifting. He said we would know them by their fruit, by the way they live, love, lead, and treat people behind closed doors. A true prophetic voice will always reflect the character of Christ. A false one will always reveal itself through lack of good fruit. We are given reminders throughout Scriptures that there will arise false prophets, false teachers, and even doctrines of devils. Their teachings look spiritual on the surface but quietly lead hearts away from the simplicity of Christ, toward confusion, fear, control, or self-exaltation. These counterfeit voices often carry a sparkle, sensation, and a promise that feeds the flesh. Real biblical prophecy is never about elevating the speaker; it is about glorifying the Father. This is written in love for you; God *still* speaks, warns, comforts, corrects, and reveals. God *still* uses His people in prophetic ways but also calls us to be wise, anchored in Scripture, and alert to anything that contradicts the Word, no matter how convincing or popular it may appear. Love is the atmosphere where prophecy and discernment both thrive. As you continue this chapter and the journey of this book, may the Father give you eyes to see, ears to hear, and a heart that clings tightly to what is the absolute truth.

146

The Trap: Personality Overshadows Fruit

One of the greatest deceptions in the modern *Big Corrupt Church* is the belief that a person's charisma equals God's anointing. We live in a generation where bold personalities, loud voices, and emotional atmospheres often draw crowds faster than quiet faithfulness, humility, or true biblical character. People rush toward the most dynamic stage, wildest worship set, and most energetic preacher, and assume that movement equals the presence of God. Jesus never told us to measure a ministry by motion; we are to measure it by its fruit. It is possible to have a booming voice, a magnetic personality, and a viral ministry while still being spiritually bankrupt. The altar is full of broken hearts, the band plays louder, and the preacher shakes the microphone, but the tree behind the stage is already rotten at the roots. Crowds are not confirmation, emotion is not evidence, and noise is not the same thing as nurture.

In many churches today, people flock to leaders who can stir a room, but they never stop long enough to examine the fruit the leader's life actually produces. They assume that because someone can prophesy, preach, pray in tongues, or generate excitement, they must be truly anointed. Charisma can be imitated, gifting can be performed, and an atmosphere can be manufactured but *Fruit cannot*.

Jesus never said you will know them by their altar calls, miracles, or baptism reports. The Word states, *"You will know them by their fruit."* Good or bad, the fruit tells it all (joy, love, peace, patience, kindness, gentleness, faithfulness, goodness, and self-control). These are our Heavenly Father's fruit.

Discernment Meets Reality

There comes a point in every believer's life when the pages of Scripture are no longer distant stories; they become a mirror. The warnings Jesus gave about wolves dressed in sheep's clothing, false signs, doctrines of devils, and lips that honor Him while hearts drift far away, suddenly stop sounding theoretical and begin to sound painfully familiar. That is where we found ourselves in the final stretch before we unplugged from our Ex-church. It was not one moment or one offense, it was the slow aching realization that what looked prophetic on the surface was actually shaped by fear, insecurity, and spiritual manipulation. We had spent years serving, believing, and pouring our hearts into this place, only to slowly wake up to the uncomfortable truth that not every voice behind a pulpit speaks from the throne room of God, no matter how confident they claim to be.

This section of my story is not written to humiliate anyone. It is written in love, with trembling hands, because silence has a cost and that cost is the next unsuspecting soul who walks through those doors thinking what they are hearing is holy. I want you, the reader, to feel the weight of what we saw, not to generate anger toward a person but to cultivate discernment toward patterns that Jesus warned us would appear in the last days. What we witnessed was not just emotional preaching, poor judgment, or immaturity; it was the misuse of the prophetic gift; twisting of spiritual authority, and confusing demonic whispers with the voice of God Himself. Truthfully, we had our own shortcomings, stayed longer than we should have, softened our convictions, and ignored the Holy Spirit in hopes of avoiding conflict. After these events occurred, we were already quietly making plans to leave; we were awake but still stuck. This is where our story turns from teaching to testimony, warnings to lived experience, and biblical principles to the very moments that tested our obedience and opened our eyes. What you are about to read is not exaggerated, embellished, or written with bitterness; it is written with reverence because these are the kinds of moments Jesus told us to watch for. Once you see them clearly, you cannot unsee them. Now, let me take you into the room with us, staff meetings, late nights, prophecies, and moments where discernment began to whisper the truth we could no longer ignore.

Discernment Finally Spoke

In the final months of our time at this ministry, something shifted; subtly at first, then unmistakably. What once felt like spiritual intensity began to feel like false spirituality. What once sounded prophetic began to echo with something far different. In that tension, between what we hoped was true and what we were actually witnessing, the Holy Spirit began to pull back the curtain. It started in a staff meeting, the kind we had sat through countless times before. It was a normal day in the office until the wolf's wife, the false prophetess, began to speak. She told us she had not slept the night before. It was not because she was praying or wrestling with God but because she claimed she had been up all night listening to the accusations from the enemy in the Throne Room of God about every single person in the church.

The false prophetess described hearing audible voices, whispers she insisted were demonic accusations directed at members of the staff. She said these voices were so loud that she had to check her phone multiple times to check the security cameras around the property, thinking someone was in her home speaking to her. She stated she wasn't fearful and never rebuked these voices. The false prophetess sat and listened to them all night for hours and was gathering information about the people around her. In a moment meant to sound spiritual but felt deeply alarming, she told us that she knew what was *"triggering"* every person in the room. The false prophetess asked us to raise our hands if we had been triggered recently and many people did. Then she laughed and said, ***"Oh, I know!"*** Those words, spoken with amusement, hit the room like a cold wind. It was not compassion or discernment; it was something else, something that made the hair on the back of our necks stand. She stated that the enemy was trying to get her to go back into her old ways of life and she knew the enemy was trying to do the same to her staff. The false prophetess even claimed that some of us had gone back to our old ways of living. She never prayed for us or asked if we needed counseling; just laughed.

The next evening was Wednesday service and the false prophetess was preaching. Her message was on the accusations of the enemy and how Satan whispers, lies, and torments. What she neglected to tell the congregation was that she had spent the previous night listening to familiar spirits, those demonic voices, whispering and assigning them to people in the room. Then she began to prophesy falsely, not words of comfort, edification, or Scripture that points people toward repentance. The performance began as the false prophetess started targeting individuals, calling out struggles, exposing supposed intentions, and speaking as if she had stood in the courts of Heaven and overheard God Himself discussing their lives. This is nonsense, lies straight from hell itself.

One couple in particular sat in the front as she declared publicly that the Lord told her they were planning to leave the church. There was no encouragement, mercy, or invitation to restoration, just a blunt accusation spoken under the guise of Godly insight. The false prophetess was not concerned with their spiritual condition; she was concerned that they had been discussing leaving the church. She then made it a point to make the couple aware that she knew their discussions.

In my personal opinion of this situation, she said she was hearing the enemy's accusations in the throne room of God. Yet what she was actually doing was listening to monitoring spirits (this is the practice of satanic witchcraft to send out spirits to monitor people, landmarks, etc.) and presenting their whispers as the voice of God through prophecy. The people, unaware, received it as the voice of God. That alone should have been enough to stop us in our tracks, but it was only the beginning.

In another staff meeting, she shared something entirely different. The false prophetess opened up about what she had been learning in Scripture that week. It was rich, beautiful truths that genuinely inspired those of us listening. We were encouraged and hopeful. It sounded like growth, revelation, and as if the Lord was genuinely teaching her. The hope did not last long.

Later on, during a Sunday service, she stepped off of the stage and began to prophesy over each of the children that were up at the altar. The false prophetess walked up to a young man on the other side of the room and began to speak word for word what she had told us in the staff meeting. Verbatim as if this was a fresh, heavenly downloaded word written just for him. She presented her personal study as if it were God's direct, unique revelation over his life. It was not prophetic, spirit led, or divine. It was rehearsed and pathetic. All of us on staff knew the truth. Kasey and I looked across the room at each other. The clapping from the congregation only made the moment heavier for us because they did not know but we did. This was not the gift of prophecy but a performance. By this time, we were already quietly planning our exit, taking steps to leave, and waking up to the truth, but we were still afraid to confront it fully. We saw the red flags, yet we stayed longer than we should have.

False Prophetess Claim to Find Staff

Here is another moment that marked a turning point. It happened during a staff meeting but not just any meeting. This was one we entered already knowing that people were going to be fired. The false prophetess had made that perfectly clear in the weeks leading up to it. For nearly two full weeks, she warned us repeatedly that some staff members *"would not make it into the next season"* of the ministry. The tension leading up to that meeting was suffocating. The emotional exhaustion was overwhelming. Every day felt like we were walking on eggshells, unsure of who would be removed, or what was coming next. The atmosphere was thick, stressful, and intensely fear filled, a level of pressure no one serving in the house of God should ever experience. On this particular day, the false prophetess began prophesying to the team again, but her tone carried a strange intensity. She described, in unsettling detail, how she had been *"finding"* each of us in the spirit realm (astral projecting). The false prophetess explained that she had gone before the Lord to see where each staff member stood spiritually, what our condition was before God, and what was happening in our private time with Him. She said she had been able to *"find"* us one by one, in the spirit realm. She spoke about who was tired, drifting, struggling, and who was still standing strong. It did not sound like biblical prophecy at all; it sounded like spiritual surveillance.

As the false prophetess continued, the staff members intently listened to every word. Each of us sat quietly waiting to hear what she would claim to have seen about our lives. For a moment, I believe she thought it would bring edification, but it caused stress and made people question themselves. This was not encouragement; it was something meant to elevate her as the one who *"knew"* more about our spiritual state than we did ourselves. The false prophetess stopped speaking, looked directly at me, and said, *"Justin, I couldn't find you in the spirit and the Lord showed me, it's because you are His man."* The room fell silent. At first, it made me self-conscious. I felt as if there was something wrong with me, but I realize now, it was the Lord's protection over my life. He did not allow her to find me in the spirit. Could my hedge of protection have possibly been the prayers petitioned for me by my family and friends? I am not entirely sure, but I am very thankful. I had never heard anyone speak this way or a Christian leader talk about *"finding people in the spirit,"* seeing them in their prayer closets, or watching them in their homes doing Bible studies. Nothing aligned with the prophetic model according to the Word of God or reflected the character of the Holy Spirit. The concept itself unsettled me. At the time, I didn't have the words for it, but something inside me felt disturbed. It took months of prayer, searching Scripture, testing everything I had seen, and asking the Lord for clarity before the truth became clear. The false prophetess described locating people spiritually, observing them in their private devotion, and claiming to track their inner condition from afar. This is not sound Biblical Doctrine but an occult like practice. It mirrored practices rooted in astral projection, New Age Mysticism, and occult like counterfeits that imitate revelation while drawing hearts away from the Holy Spirit. These are not tools of discernment; they are distortions of witchcraft that give a leader a false sense of prophetic abilities. She used this craft to establish dominance, make us feel as though she had superior access to the kingdom of God, and to create a fear that she could see what we could not. If the false prophetess could *"find"* us in the spirit, see our prayer life, or watch us in our homes, what would be next? It was spiritual intimidation wrapped in religious language and a counterfeit spirituality designed to control us rather than to edify. We did not realize the full weight of it at first, understand what we were actually witnessing, or have the courage to label it for what it truly was. Now looking back, after prayer, deliverance, study, and the gentle correction of the Holy Spirit, we can clearly see this was not Godly prophecy. It was a dangerous mixture of occult like practices that have no place in the house of God.

Prophecy Became Prediction

The wolf also had his own moments of *"prophecy"* from the pulpit, moments that carried weight, urgency, and an atmosphere of fear more than faith. He often stated boldly that if a person gets one prophecy wrong, they are by his definition, a *"false prophet."* The wolf preached it firmly, repeated it often, and laid it down like an unbreakable spiritual law. The standard he held over everyone else never seemed to hold the same weight for him or his wife, the false prophetess. Throughout our years serving under the wolf, he released many false prophetic declarations; some small, some dramatic, but a few stood out during the 2024 election season. The wolf stood before the congregation and proclaimed in the name of the Spirit of God that Verizon Wireless was going to shut down all communication before the election; that was false. He said food shortages were imminent; that was false also.

The wolf even said that everything was going to be shut down just like it was during Covid; that was false as well. He positioned these claims as urgent and divine warnings, not possibilities, concerns, or prophecies. That lying wolf declared that our church would be a safe haven when the world shuts down again and our building would be open while others would be closed. He said God told him people would come to us for refuge, help, and safety when everything collapsed. The wolf spoke with such confidence that the room hung on every word. He urged us to get the message out before the chaos began, implying that we were being entrusted with inside information from Heaven itself.

As of December 2025, not one of those words came to pass, no massive communication blackouts, food shortages or shutdowns. None of the prophetic warnings unfolded, not even partially. By the wolf's own standard, preached from the pulpit, a single failed prophecy disqualifies anyone from speaking for God. According to the words he and his wife proclaimed, that same standard indicts them both and exposes the many prophecies he delivered that were later proven false. False prophecy does not just damage credibility; it damages people, manipulates emotions, creates fear, turns leaders into spiritual authorities they were never meant to be, and convinces congregations that God has spoken when God has not. When Biblical prophecy is replaced with prediction, fear is disguised as discernment, pastors speak their anxieties as if they are the voice of the Lord, and the manner of fruit will always reveal itself in time and it did. This is one more piece of the story that opened our eyes to the reality of what we were living under.

Prophetic Warning: Not from God

There are so many examples that I could give you on
this topic, but for the sake of time and to be honoring, I
will only speak on instances that really stand out in my
memory. There is another moment that occurred earlier
in the ministry that left me confused, unsettled, and
questioning everything I thought I knew about
prophetic voices. It happened late one afternoon in our
office building. We were gathering our things, getting
ready to head home, when one of our *"house prophets"*
(a familiar voice to the church world) stepped toward us
with a seriousness I had never seen in him before. He
stood by the door and asked if he could have a word
with me. He looked straight into my eyes intently and
said, *"Justin, you are a Bible man. What the Bible says,
you stick to it, but I want to tell you, your pastor is a
man of God. Don't leave."* The words hit me strangely
as if they didn't belong in the moment. At that time,
leaving the church was not even a thought in my mind.
I was not questioning leadership, planning an exit, or
doubting our direction. I was wholeheartedly serving
and believing we were doing everything we could to
follow Scripture, honor God, and walk in obedience to
our leaders. His warning felt completely out of place,
like a key trying to fit a lock that didn't exist yet. I
remember standing there, confused, replaying his words
in my mind as we walked out the door. Don't leave,
your pastor is a man of God and look past what you see.
Why would he say something like that or claimed to
hear from God to give me a warning I did not need?
What I could not see then; is what I can see with clarity
now, this was a *"$ profit $ word"* not prophetic. It was
a spiritual nudge meant to keep me loyal to those he
was receiving payment from in the ministry partnership
with suppressing discernment and anchor me to a

system that the Holy Spirit Himself was already preparing to lead us out of.

Here is the truth my friends, the Lord Himself was the one who eventually told me to leave, write this book, and exposed what was happening in the shadows. So why would a prophetic voice, someone who claimed to hear from the mouth of God, tell me the exact opposite of what the Lord would later confirm to my spirit with undeniable clarity? This was a *"charismatic $ profit $"* standing in front of me who cared about his money, urging me to stay, inadvertently urging me to look past the Bible, discernment, red flags that were to come, and remain loyal no matter what I saw or felt. This *"charismatic $profit$"* told me to trust his word more than the Word of God: *"God is not a man, that he should lie; neither the son of man, that he should repent..."* **(Numbers 23:19 KJV)**. God does not contradict Himself, lead through confusion, or ask His people to ignore Scripture. He never calls us to remain where His Word exposes error. Looking back, that encounter was not confirmation; it was manipulation wrapped in spiritual language, a warning not from Heaven but from a system losing its grip. Any prophetic voice that asks you to ignore Scripture, suppress discernment, or silence the Holy Spirit is not speaking for God, no matter how sincere, intense, or convincing it sounds. The voice of God never leads away from His Word, only back to it: *"As we said before, so say I now again, if any man preach any other gospel unto you than that ye have received, let him be accursed"* **(Galatians 1:9 KJV)**.

Discerning the Spirit Behind Prophecy
One of the greatest gifts God gave us through everything we endured was discernment. At first, we did not know how to test prophecy or recognize the

157

spirit behind it. We trusted the wrong voices, believing they were holy, and carried burdens we were never meant to bear. Yet, God did not condemn us, He taught us and opened our eyes through Scripture, patience, and truth. Missing the signs does not make you weak in faith, naïve, or foolish. It means you had a tender heart that wanted to honor God. The Lord does not shame people for trusting deeply; He teaches them how to trust wisely. Over time, God showed us how to test what is spoken by its fruit and His Word. True prophecy draws people closer to Jesus that aligns with Scripture, produces peace, and reflects Christ's character. Anything that confuses, controls, elevates the speaker, or contradicts the Bible, no matter how emotional or convincing, must be *rejected*. We share this not to attack the prophetic but to protect it. Prophecy is real. The Holy Spirit still speaks; God equips His people to recognize counterfeits before they cause harm. Discernment anchored in the Word leads to freedom, clarity, and trust restored in Him alone.

Healing from Abused Prophetic Words

Few wounds in the church are as disorienting as realizing that something spoken *"in the name of the Lord"* did not come from Him. When prophecy turns poisonous, it does more than mislead; it steals peace, fractures trust, redirects lives, and burdens souls with expectations God never placed. Scripture never treats prophecy as unquestionable; it commands us to test it (*1 John 4:1* KJV). When prophecy is placed beyond discernment, it stops serving God's people and begins ruling them.

Poisonous prophecy often disguises itself as urgency, using fear to force compliance. Yet God's voice does not produce confusion or panic but peace (*1 Corinthians 14:33* KJV). Any word that creates anxiety, condemnation, or dependence on the speaker, bears fruit God does not produce. Jesus said, *"My sheep hear my voice"* (**John 10:27** KJV) not through control or intermediaries (anything or anyone that stands where only Jesus should stand) but through relationship.

The Bible is clear that prophecy must be weighed, not swallowed whole (**1 Corinthians 14:29** KJV). God does not trap His children through coercive or unclear words, nor does He hinge their future on one moment or one person. Even in Scripture, prophecy was often conditional and subject to mercy, revealing that God's character always governs His words.

Healing comes by releasing words that never bore good fruit. Jesus taught that every tree is known by its fruit (**Luke 6:44** KJV). God is not offended when His people let go of false prophecy or threatened by discernment. His wisdom is pure, peaceable, and gentle (**James 3:17** KJV). As trust is restored, believers learn again to recognize the difference between pressure and peace as well as manipulation and invitation.

Prophecy's rightful place is not a weapon or throne but a gift meant to edify, exhort, and comfort (**1 Corinthians 14:3** KJV). You did not fail God because someone spoke falsely or missed His will because a word was wrong. God's voice remains gentle, faithful, and trustworthy; He is fully able to lead His people forward without fear, confusion, or words He never spoke.

Chapter 10
The Double Life of the Pulpit

God makes it clear in Scripture that those who stand before His people bear a weight unlike any other. Teaching the Word of God is not a career, platform, or performance; it is a sacred stewardship. James warns that *"not many should become teachers,"* because teachers will be judged more strictly. Jesus Himself rebuked the religious leaders of His day not because they taught the Scriptures but because *they refused to live what they taught.* He said they tied up heavy burdens, yokes impossible to carry, and laid them on the shoulders of the people, yet they would not lift one finger to help bear them. The problem was not their preaching; it was their hypocrisy.

Throughout Scripture, pastors are called to lead by example, not intimidation. Biblical authority flows from a life aligned with the message, not from words used to excuse behavior. When leaders preach holiness but refuse to walk in it, demand submission they do not model, or place burdens on others they will not carry themselves, the foundation of the church is damaged. Teaching matters because it shapes lives. When the pulpit reflects Jesus, people flourish; when it contradicts Him, people are wounded. This is written not to condemn leaders, but to call pastors and people alike back to Christ where authority is given through humility. Teaching is stewardship and God's Word is carried by example, not imposed by force.

As the years unfolded, I began to realize that the teachings we sat under were shaping far more than our Sundays, they were shaping our decisions, relationships, identities, and even our understanding of God Himself. Week after week, the pulpit became the loudest voice in our lives and without realizing it, we absorbed doctrines that guided how we thought, lived, and treated those around us. At first, everything sounded biblical, passionate, and purposeful, but slowly, almost imperceptibly, the tone began to shift. Messages that once seemed rooted in Scripture started drifting into control, fear, and contradiction. The very teachings that claimed to bring freedom began to place chains on our hearts. It was not one sermon or one moment, it was a pattern that emerged over time, woven into the rhythm of the ministry. What followed were the teachings that shaped us, doctrines we lived under, and truths we eventually had to unlearn in order to return to the heart of Jesus.

In 2025, something in our church shifted, quietly at first, then loudly, then all consumingly. Our former pastors, the wolf and false prophetess, began to rally around one of our house values with more intensity than anything I had ever seen, *"habitation."* If you had asked me then, I would have told you it was one of the most beautiful things our church had ever embraced. At least, that's what I thought in the beginning. Biblically, the idea is breathtaking. The Scriptures say God does not dwell in temples made with human hands. Paul goes even further to say, *"we; fragile, flawed, ordinary people; are the temple of the Holy Spirit."* That truth brings tears to my eyes. The Creator of the Universe has chosen to make His home in us; not in concrete, drywall, a stage or in a building made by hands. Truthfully when *"habitation"* was first introduced in staff meetings, that's exactly what it felt like, pure, humble, and hopeful. We talked about wanting God to dwell among us as a body of believers. We prayed, not for crowds or influence but for Him. I remember feeling a spark inside me, almost like, *"Yes, Lord. Let this be real and holy."* However, somewhere between those meetings and the Sunday sermons, the meaning started to mutate. Little by little, the message began to shift from *"God dwells in His people"* to *"God dwells in this house."* At first, I thought I was imagining it, just a few phrases that felt off, but then it became consistent, bold, and territorial. Suddenly our former pastors, the wolf and the false prophetess, were teaching that our church was the only place where God lived, deliverance and healing took place, and *"real salvation"* was received. The unspoken (and sometimes spoken) implication was, if you're not in our building, you're missing what God is doing.

The first time it hit me like a punch was when I was publicly rebuked from the pulpit, my name was not said, but everyone who needed to know, knew my *"offense."* I had told people online the truth, that God could deliver them anywhere and His power was not bound to a physical location; the Holy Spirit does not check addresses. The wolf said otherwise; he declared that our property and sanctuary was a *"glory hole where God dwelt."* I remember sitting in my seat, my heart sinking into my stomach, thinking, *"When did we start believing we owned the presence of God?"* Then came the sign over the church doors, ***"Welcome to His Habitation."*** It felt like we were branding something sacred and claiming something that was never ours to claim. Prayer meetings became centered around the building itself. They prayed for people to come, not to meet Jesus wherever they were but to step into *our* sanctuary, as though God's presence stopped at county lines or refused to travel down the street. Rarely did I hear the truth the Bible so clearly states that His habitation is in His people, their homes, workplaces, quiet places, tears, and repentance. This was a message

162

the wolf repeated numerous times, *"If you 're not in our church, you are not experiencing God's fullness."* If anyone dared to suggest otherwise, they were considered disloyal, rebellious, or out of alignment. That's when the ache started because I could feel the beauty slipping away. The thing that started pure was becoming a tool or another way to make the church feel indispensable, irreplaceable, or superior. It was a way to bind people to the church, not truly set them free. Looking back, the pattern is unmistakably manipulation disguised as uniqueness, exclusivity preached as holiness, and quiet indoctrination that framed our church as *"chosen"* in a way no other church was. Leaving was portrayed not as a choice but as betrayal of God's will. What was meant to lead people into God's presence, instead redirected their allegiance to a building, brand, and a man-made system. What should have brought freedom became a tool of control. What should have united the body of Christ created an invisible wall between *"us"* and *"everyone else."* That's what makes this so devastating. It did not seem this way to us in the beginning. It began with sincerity, Scripture, and a genuine hunger for God. Somewhere along the way, the focus shifted from belonging to God to possessing Him as if God belonged to the system, rather than the system belonging to God.

Stewardship

Stewardship was a constant theme in our church. We were taught that faithfulness with little, leads to greater trust, and generosity brings blessing. The teaching itself was Biblically sound. Scripture does call us to steward God's resources with integrity and I will continue to believe that. The heartbreak came in discovering the widening gap between what was preached and what was practiced. Stewardship in Scripture is sacred, not

163

sensational. It demands accountability, not theatrics. Jesus taught that how we handle money, people, time, and influence reveals the true condition of the heart. God does not bless waste, deception, or ego-driven leadership disguised as generosity. Once you see that gap, you cannot unsee it. We spoke openly about faithfulness inside the church, but behind the scenes, I witnessed things that are still difficult to reconcile.

The Gifts No One Saw Again

People would bring gifts, handwritten letters, small tokens of love, and thoughtful items they felt prompted by the Lord to give. I watched our former pastors, the wolf and false prophetess, open envelopes only to check for money, then toss the letter and the gift into the trash without even reading them. I saw gifts for our former pastors, the wolf and false prophetess, thrown away unopened just tossed aside and notes of gratitude and prayer were discarded like junk mail. I still remember standing there, stunned, when I was handed gifts that were meant for them knowing they were planning to throw them away. I think about the people who prayed over those gifts before they sent them and who sowed them in faith believing they were honoring their leaders. They will never know their offering never made it past the first glance.

The Halloween Burning

The moment that branded itself into my memory happened on a night we held what was called an occult burning on Halloween. Hundreds of congregants surrounded a fire, believing they were laying down old bondage and burning symbols of their past in exchange for freedom. It was meant to be a symbolic and powerful cleansing. People came ready for breakthrough. What they did not know and only a few of us witnessed was the wolf had secretly bagged up gifts that members of that same congregation had given him and threw them into the fire right in front of them. They had no idea that the precious items they had offered in love were being burned publicly as if they were occult objects. I remember standing there, the fire popping and the crowd shouting praise, and feeling something inside me go quiet and completely still. Something felt deeply, deeply wrong.

The Dumpster

The day finally came to prepare for the move to the new building. We were assigned to clean out the old offices, sorting years of ministry items, furniture, equipment, and gifts. The false prophetess had been given a hand painted portrait of her with her husband, the wolf. It was beautiful, meaningful, and valuable, but she did not want it. Not only did she not value it, but she also wanted it buried. The false prophetess instructed us to place it at the very bottom of a large dumpster and then cover it with everything from the offices so no one would find it. When I say *"everything,"* I mean everything. We threw away hundreds, if not thousands of dollars of perfectly usable ministry materials such as chairs, tables, desks, shelves, office supplies, and unopened resources. What a waste of great materials; this is certainly not showing stewardship or thankfulness. The final act exposed everything. She ordered staff to cover the discarded gifts in the dumpster with spoiled food so no one could retrieve or even see them. The items were intentionally destroyed, not for cleanliness or stewardship but to conceal the rejection of a gift. This was not about order or gratitude; it was about protecting her image while quietly discarding the people she claimed to serve.

On Sundays, we were told God trusted this ministry because it was faithful, generous, and abundant. Sermons on giving and stewardship stirred belief that people were sowing into something holy. However, behind the scenes offerings were discarded, gifts given in love were destroyed, and resources were wasted to hide the truth. Stewardship became a performance, not a principle. I still believe in biblical stewardship, generosity, and accountability, but true stewardship is not proven by loud preaching.

Ministry Becomes Neglect

One of the hardest realities we faced during our time in leadership was witnessing how deeply poor stewardship can wound the very people a ministry is called to serve. While we were in the process of purchasing the church building and ultimately the wolf's personal home, there were nearly thirty missionaries that were suddenly and silently cut off from critical financial support. These were not casual partnerships; they were ministries that depended on our church to survive. Many of them functioned month to month on the support we had promised them. Yet not a single one received any warning, explanation, or even a courtesy message letting them know their funding was ending. They simply stopped receiving help. The heartbreaking part is that these missionaries began calling the church, confused, concerned, and desperate for answers. They were not calling to complain but simply calling because their ability to minister, feed their families, and continuing the work of the Gospel depended on the support we had pledged. I was instructed to ignore them, not to answer their questions, offer clarity, or explain the sudden cutoff. I was not told why they were no longer receiving funding. I sat there hearing the phone ring, knowing brothers and sisters in Christ were serving in difficult countries, relying on our faithfulness, and being left in the dark with no answers. One gentleman in particular called repeatedly trying to understand what had happened. Instead of concern or compassion, the false prophetess dismissed him, calling him rude and demanding. She said she was *"done with him."*

To this day, I don't believe many of these ministries ever learned why their support vanished without warning. As someone who answered that phone, heard the confusion and hurt in their voices, this remains one of the deepest wounds in my spirit. This is not biblical stewardship and honoring the laborers in the harvest. Scripture commands us to provide for those who minister, give generously, keep our word, and steward resources with integrity, transparency, and fear of the Lord. Instead of our leadership treating these missionaries with dignity and truthfulness, they were abandoned without explanation so that larger personal projects could move forward. Good stewardship is not about large purchases or impressive buildings; it is about faithfulness, keeping commitments, and honoring those who serve Christ around the world. When the church stops caring for the ones laboring on the front lines, it ceases to reflect the heart of the One who sent them.

Living What We Preach

Scripture is clear, those who preach the Word are called to live it. The Bible never separates proclamation from practice and Jesus warned that spiritual authority becomes dangerous when leaders place burdens on others they refuse to carry themselves. Biblical leadership is not performance but demonstration; credibility comes not from eloquence but from example. When the message preached on Sunday does not match the life lived in private, the people suffer. Trust erodes, confusion grows, and what should bring clarity, instead brings harm. That is why what we witnessed was so devastating; the principles used to correct the congregation were not applied to leadership. In the moments ahead, we will share what we saw where preaching gave way to performance and God began to expose the difference.

Preach One Thing but Live Another

One of the messages the wolf returned to repeatedly was the command to *"get your house in order."* It became a defining theme of his preaching, a call to holiness, discipline, and spiritual seriousness. On its face, the message was Biblical: *"But I keep under my body, and bring it into subjection: lest that by any means, when I have preached to others, I myself should be a castaway"* **(1 Corinthians 9:27 KJV)**. Scripture does call believers to steward their homes with integrity and wisdom. We believed that and lived that. In ministry, we walked with families through addiction, rebellion, confusion, and heartbreak knowing that none of us walk perfectly with God.

What shattered us was discovering that the standard preached from the pulpit did not apply behind the scenes. While the congregation was warned that drug use in the home *"invited devils,"* the wolf's own son openly used drugs in their house, overdosed, and entered rehab multiple times. Another son actively used and sold drugs on church property without consequence. While medication was publicly condemned as *"the spirit of Pharmakeia,"* the pastoral family privately relied on Suboxone and other prescriptions. While secular music was preached against as demonic, their children listened freely, engaged in sexual activity on church property, and used

168

drugs during service times. At the same time, the congregation was instructed to cleanse their homes, remove family members, sever relationships, and purge possessions deemed spiritually unsafe. People obeyed not out of fear but out of sincere devotion to God. Families were divided, loved ones were removed from homes, heirlooms were discarded, and relationships were sacrificed, all under teachings that leadership themselves refused to live by. The rules were strict for the people and nonexistent for those in authority. The wolf openly encouraged members to cut off family who questioned the ministry, assuring them the church would become their new family, but this was not relationship; it was ideology, loyalty demanded, not love offered. We watched people isolate themselves fearful of their own parents and siblings, convinced that family ties were spiritual threats. Yet none of these standards were enforced within leadership. It was hypocrisy cloaked in holiness and bondage disguised as Biblical instruction.

This is what happens when preaching becomes performance instead of practice and when leaders demand from others what they refuse to carry themselves. Jesus warned about this and we watched it unfold in real time. It was this undeniable disconnect between what was preached and what was lived that finally exposed what was truly operating within the ministry.

Protecting Your Peace Dishonorably

One teaching that shaped me more than I ever realized and wounded my family more than I ever intended, was the constant pulpit message that it was *"holy"* to cut people out of your life. Week after week, we heard that anyone who disagreed with our spiritual choices was a threat to our peace, distraction to our calling, or an open door to the enemy. The pulpit taught that family members who questioned the ministry were *"hindrances"* and honoring God meant blocking out anyone who didn't celebrate what we were doing. I believed, absorbed, and lived it without ever realizing the damage it would cause.

My family was not happy when we moved to Tennessee. They did not like the church; they certainly did not trust our former pastors, the wolf and false prophetess. Instead of slowing down, listening, praying, or weighing their concerns biblically, I was taught to harden myself, treat their warnings as spiritual attacks, and let go of anyone who stood in the way of God. I swallowed that doctrine whole. I pushed them aside, shut them out, minimized their voices, and believed that cutting them off was honoring Jesus. I want to say this plainly, *I was wrong*, not just a little wrong but devastatingly, sinfully, and heartbreakingly wrong. God does not want us to despise those who raised, loved, prayed, and sacrificed for us. Give honor where honor is due. My family still suffers from the ripple effect of those teachings.

Four years had gone by since I sat at a table with my side of the family and shared a meal. There were four years of missed birthdays, holidays, ordinary days, and moments with my grandparents, gone until Thanksgiving of 2025. I helped create those four years of silence by choosing the voice of a pulpit over the voices of the people who loved me before anyone in the church even knew my name. My parents and my sister still do not speak to me because of my past affiliation with that church. I want the reader to feel the weight of that, not for sympathy but for truth. When a pulpit teaches you to discard people, it is not preaching Jesus. When a pastor tells you to *"protect your peace"* by cutting off anyone who disagrees with them, they are not teaching the gospel. They are teaching isolation, control, and fear. True peace is not found in severing the people God gave you; it is found in walking in humility, reconciliation, and truth. With all sincerity, I want to publicly repent to God. I also want to repent to my family for:

- shutting you out
- believing a man's voice over your love
- treating your concern as an attack
- letting doctrine distort my discernment
- choosing loyalty to a ministry over loyalty to the people who shaped my life
- the holidays missed, conversations ignored, and wounds I caused
- letting pride, fear, and spiritual manipulation harden my heart against the very people God commanded me to honor

If you were taught to abandon family or relationships in the name of spiritual growth, hear this clearly, that is not the way of Christ. The Shepherd who leaves the ninety-nine does not teach His people to discard the ones closest to them. God calls us to reconciliation, not isolation. True peace is not found in cutting people off but in Jesus restoring what false teaching tried to destroy. I am still rebuilding what I allowed to crumble, choosing restoration over isolation and Scripture over the ease of separation because the voice of God always brings people together, never tears them apart.

Weaponized Unity

Unity was not encouraged in our church; it was enforced. It was preached as the highest virtue, while disagreement was labeled rebellion and questioning leadership equated with resisting God. Yet behind the pulpit, the very leaders who condemned *"division"* fueled gossip and discord themselves. Unity became a weapon used to silence accountability while protecting those in power.

This is where Thomas's story resurfaces. Do you remember him from the beginning of this book? Thomas was once incredibly close to the wolf. They rode bikes and traveled together. They also spent long hours in ministry planning. At one point, Thomas asked the false prophetess if he could purchase equipment to start a men's podcast. She approved it without hesitation, *"Get whatever you need,"* she said. Not long after the purchase, everything shifted. I received a call from the false prophetess insisting she was *100% certain* Thomas was sabotaging the ministry financially. The accusations had no proof, context, or biblical grounding, but they were presented as divine revelation. They placed Thomas in positions of immense responsibility such as handling court matters for the church and representing the ministry before the county yet provided no guidance or support. Then in a manipulative conversation, the false prophetess told me that the Lord had revealed to her that we would *not* enter a new building until Thomas was gone. She blamed him for the delays insisting he was the spiritual barrier preventing progress. Thomas was not fired and we still moved into the building, disproving every prophetic accusation she had made.

This type of manipulation was constant. Staff members were pitted against one another like pieces on a chessboard. We were pressured into confronting, disciplining, or firing each other with no biblical process or pastoral care. The staff was instructed to report on one another's conversations, behaviors, and private frustrations to the false prophetess. It created an environment of paranoia, secrecy, and psychological distress. Firing threats were woven into normal conversation. We were told constantly that the church was under financial strain and that staff cuts were necessary. Many loved staff members were let go because of false statements about finances. Even Thomas's wife was let go. At one point, out of loyalty, I willingly surrendered a portion of my pay to *"help the church."* Months later, the false prophetess told me we were never struggling financially but simply needed a reason to get rid of certain staff members. She still took my pay; I spent the next seven months without part of my paycheck because of a lie. That level of emotional manipulation became normal. Every staff member was told privately they were safe, valued, and not the one in danger of being fired, but *"everyone else"* was. Only later did we discover this was said to every single staff member. The goal was to isolate us from one another, destroy trust, and secure loyalty through fear. To make matters worse, favoritism was wielded like a weapon. The false prophetess frequently took select groups of women on church funded outings, getting their nails done, going out to eat, and even taking a group to the Smoky Mountains, while intentionally leaving certain staff women behind. The exclusion was not accidental; it was targeted. It reinforced insecurity, desperation, and a craving for approval. To this day, the false prophetess openly declares that the worship team members are *"her children,"* insisting that the Lord Himself has placed a mandate on her to raise *them* up in the ministry, disciple *them*, and ensure that *they* move forward spiritually. She made it abundantly clear that this responsibility did not extend to the rest of us. The false prophetess told the staff repeatedly that it was not her mandate to disciple, mentor, or equip us. That calling she said, belonged only to the worship team. The message was unmistakable; some people mattered and others did not. Some were chosen and others were

173

expendable. In a church culture where unity was preached aggressively from the pulpit, this kind of favoritism created a hierarchical system that fractured the staff emotionally. Those not in her inner circle were made to feel spiritually inferior, overlooked, and unworthy of development. It reinforced the idea that value was not rooted in Christ but in access to her approval, attention, and definition of calling.

The psychological impact of being told you are **not** worth discipling, while watching others elevated simply because they were favored, was devastating and profoundly confusing for those trying to serve faithfully in the house of God. This kind of psychological damage does not fully register while you're living through it. You're too busy trying to survive, stay in good standing, and avoid being the next person pushed out. In the four years I served, nineteen staff members were hired, fired, or resigned. Nearly everyone that grew close to the wolf and false prophetess, saw the truth hidden behind the curtain and eventually left while being publicly berated from the stage. No concerns, questions, or healthy communication were allowed. We were forbidden to talk about conflict outside of staff meetings.

Recently, after another staff member was let go, I spoke with them on the phone. They said repeatedly, *"I'm not crazy. This happened to me. I'm not crazy. I saw this happen."* Their words summed up what we felt; the gaslighting was so deep, constant, and pervasive that we questioned our own sanity. We questioned whether what we were experiencing was real or imagined, but it was real. This is why our story must be told with truthfulness, clarity, and courage. It is to prevent anyone else from mistaking manipulation for unity or abuse for leadership ever again.

Apology to the Staff

I want to apologize to every staff member who served alongside us during the past four years. I am sorry for not seeing or speaking up sooner, and for my silence when you needed protection. I participated in a system that exhausted, confused, and caused you to question your worth, calling, and sanity. You deserved safety, truth, and leadership that nurtured rather than controlled. Many of us are still grieving and healing, but we are no longer willing to ignore what God was trying to show us. You are valued, worthy of protection, and deserve to walk in truth.

Reflection and Healing

Looking back, one truth remains steady; Jesus is still the Good Shepherd and His heart has never changed. Even when leaders fail and Scripture is misused, He remains gentle, faithful, and free of fear or control. This season taught us that His voice is different, bringing life, restoring dignity, and freeing rather than binding. Discernment did not come through suspicion but through knowing His character so well that counterfeits became clear. Jesus never separates truth from love or holiness from humility. He does not burden His people, divide families, or use doctrine to control but invites us to walk humbly, examine our own hearts, and allow His Word to heal what misuse once harmed. I pray you are led back to the safety of Christ's heart, a Shepherd who heals gently, leads faithfully, and continues restoring what was wounded.

When holiness is demanded but not demonstrated, it becomes a weapon, not a witness. Leaders who impose standards they refuse to live turn God's truth into control, leaving believers burdened, ashamed, and confused. Jesus condemned this hypocrisy of placing heavy yokes on others while excusing themselves. Scripture makes clear that God's standards are not selective. Rejecting that distortion is not rejecting holiness; it is refusing abuse masquerading as obedience.

Chapter 11
Religious Persecution
Red Flag: **The Dangers of False Persecution**

Discerning Correction from Persecution

Scripture treats persecution as sacred but specific. It is suffering for Christ's sake, not for pride, misconduct, or refusal to repent. Jesus said, *"Blessed are they which are persecuted for righteousness' sake... Blessed are ye, when men shall revile you, and persecute you... for my sake"* (**Matthew 5:10–11 KJV**). He did not bless those confronted for their behavior. When correction, accountability, or consequences are mislabeled as persecution, truth is distorted and repentance is silenced. Peter warned the church plainly, *"But let none of you suffer as a murderer, or as a thief, or as an evildoer, or as a busybody in other men's matters"* (**1 Peter 4:15 KJV**). This misuse is spiritually dangerous because it shields wrongdoing, recasts victims as enemies, and allows leaders to claim martyrdom while avoiding responsibility. What we witnessed was not persecution for faithfulness; it was accountability reframed as an attack, and correction dismissed as spiritual warfare.

I could no longer ignore the pattern I was seeing. The language of persecution was being used to silence truth, not uphold it. It protected authority rather than purity and influence rather than integrity. As uncomfortable realities surfaced, the narrative intensified that we were being *"opposed"* for Christ's sake, yet the fruit told a different story. Jesus said plainly, *"Ye shall know them by their fruits"* (**Matthew 7:16 KJV**). What I witnessed was not the biblical suffering of righteous believers standing firm in faith but the misuse of Scripture to deflect accountability and disguise what was happening behind the scenes. Scripture warns, *"But let none of you suffer… as an evildoer…"* (**1 Peter 4:15 KJV**). That realization marked the breaking point where conviction replaced confusion. I could no longer call it persecution when it was correction being resisted.

The Night the House Was Shot

One of the most notorious stories in the church's history was the night shots were fired into the wolf's home. It was a night filled with fear, chaos, and shock. Bullets riddled the home, glass shattered, and walls were pierced. Their son was in the home during the gunfire but was unharmed. Within hours, the story spread. By Sunday, the congregation was solemn, emotional, and shaken. The wolf and false prophetess stood before the people, voice trembling, eyes heavy, and declared that the attack came because of his bold biblical preaching, specifically his unwavering stand with Israel. He said darkness hated the truth he preached and the enemy was trying to stop the ministry for righteousess' sake. The entire church wept, people rushed to the altars, men stood to their feet in applause, and women cried into their hands. There was a collective sense that we were now part of something sacred and historic, a real modern-day persecution, like the book of Acts unfolding in our own backyard. The narrative carried weight, inspiration, and a sobering reminder that standing for truth is costly. However, behind closed doors, away from the pulpit and the livestream, the staff heard a very different story. We were told that the shooting had nothing to do with Israel, preaching, or standing for righteousness. We were told that the real reason bullets pierced the walls of that home was that their son had been selling drugs on the property, entangled with gang members, and owed them a significant amount of money. The shooting, we were told, was not persecution; it was a warning. I remember sitting there listening and feeling my stomach twist. The details were specific with no speculation. We were told plainly that the attack was connected to choices that had nothing to do with Jesus and everything to do with sin, fear, and the consequences of a dangerous lifestyle.

This moment became a turning point for me. It was the first time I witnessed the misuse of biblical language with such gravity. On one side, we had the congregation, faithful, trusting, sincere, and grieving over the idea that the wolf and false prophetess were targeted because of the Gospel. On the other side, we had the truth, that the bullets were the consequences of hidden choices, not the cost of biblical conviction. The two stories could not have been more opposite. This is what Peter warned about when he said, *"But let none of you suffer as… an evildoer"* (*1 Peter 4:15* KJV). Not all suffering is persecution; it is dangerous to pretend it is, especially from the pulpit.

Kasey and I sat in that tension, torn between compassion and concern. We were grateful the family was safe; we truly were. We love them. No one rejoiced in the danger, no one minimized the fear, and no one dismissed the seriousness of what happened. What grieved us was the narrative being spun. Scripture says, *"But he that doeth truth cometh to the light…"* (*John 3:21* KJV). Yet instead of truth coming into the light, a heroic story was presented to the people; one that made the wolf appear persecuted for righteousness when in reality, it was the consequences of private compromise. Something beautiful came from this story. This traumatic event became the very moment that eventually led their son back to the Lord. While we rejoiced that private repentance occurred with their son, a public confession should have been made to the congregation for the way the truth was misrepresented. A beautiful testimony cannot be built on a lie.

For Kasey and me, this night revealed the heart of the system we were serving under. It showed how quickly suffering could be reframed as persecution. It also revealed how easily blame could be redirected and how swiftly the congregation could be rallied around a narrative that was inspirational but not honest. This was misrepresented persecution powerfully told and emotionally gripping but spiritually misleading. This opened my eyes to how often the language of spiritual attack was used not to identify genuine persecution but to protect a story, preserve an image, and keep the congregation from asking questions they deserved answers to.

The Lawsuits

Another area where I began to recognize the confusion between persecution and personal responsibility involved the lawsuits pending against the property. From the pulpit, these actions were often described as the county and nearby residents opposing us because of our faith, framing the ministry as a victim of religious hostility. That narrative was compelling and unifying for the congregation. However, those of us on staff were aware that most of the legal actions were not related to religious expression or biblical conviction. They stemmed from building and zoning issues, specifically construction and property use that did not comply with required permits and county regulations, despite repeated warnings. When enforcement followed, it was presented publicly as persecution, though it was in fact, a consequence of noncompliance. While some neighbor concerns may reasonably be attributed to operating a large, active ministry within a residential area, the county's lawsuits were administrative and legal in nature, not an attempt to suppress the Gospel. Characterizing these matters as persecution obscured the real issue, delayed correction, and prevented truthful accountability. This was not opposition to faith but a failure to meet legal obligations and reframing it otherwise, distorting the truth rather than addressing it.

Healing from Fear Based Faith

Scripture draws a clear line between persecution for righteousness and confrontation for wrongdoing. Jesus blessed those persecuted *"...for righteousness' sake..."* **(Matthew 5:10 KJV)**, but Peter warned, *"Let none of you suffer... as an evildoer..."* **(1 Peter 4:15 KJV)**. When accountability is labeled persecution, truth is silenced and fear replaces discernment. False persecution narratives turn correction into attack and loyalty into a test of faith, isolating believers and exhausting consciences. Yet Scripture says, *"But if we walk in the light... we have fellowship one with another"* **(1 John 1:7 KJV)**. Light invites examination, only darkness demands unquestioned allegiance. True persecution does not need manipulation to be believed. The apostles *"...rejoicing that they were counted worthy to suffer shame for his name"* **(Acts 5:41 KJV)**, while God reminds us, *"But he that doeth truth cometh to the light..."* **(John 3:21 KJV)**. Questioning the light is not rebellion; it is obedience. Truth has never needed fear to stand.

Those Serving in Leadership

I want to be clear before God and before the reader. This book is not an attack on the wolf, false prophetess, or the church I once served. I have given years of my life, prayers, labor, and heart to this ministry; even now

I desire God's best for it. I love their souls but cannot love or remain silent about the contradiction of what was preached publicly and lived privately. Love that ignores hypocrisy is not love; it is abandonment. I did not write this lightly but in fear of the Lord, knowing that *"But he that doeth truth cometh to the light..."* (*John 3:21* KJV), and that *"For there is nothing covered, that shall not be revealed..."* (*Luke 12:2* KJV). This book is not meant to expose for destruction but to call for repentance, for myself first, and for those I love. I have confessed my own failures, silence, and compromise because repentance must begin in the house of God. Scripture commands me, *"And have no fellowship with the unfruitful works of darkness, but rather reprove them"* (*Ephesians 5:11* KJV). I have a responsibility to God's people and a duty to the shepherds I served to love them enough to tell the truth: *"Faithful are the wounds of a friend..."* (*Proverbs 27:6* KJV). This is not written in bitterness but in hope that humility will lead to mercy and what was once pure can yet be restored: *"Humble yourselves in the sight of the Lord, and he shall lift you up"* (*James 4:10* KJV). I say with humility and love to come back to the heart of God. Stand before the people and repent, not as one ruined but as one being restored. A repentant leader carries more authority than a defensive one and *"He that covereth his sins shall not prosper: but whoso confesseth and forsaketh them shall have mercy"* (*Proverbs 28:13* KJV). My prayer is that this book does not mark an ending but a return, not judgment but mercy. I ask the Lord to begin this work in me first, to cleanse what must be cleansed and heal what has been hidden, that we may all walk again in His light. For *"But if we walk in the light, as he is in the light... the blood of Jesus Christ his Son cleanseth us from all sin"* (*1 John 1:7* KJV). Grace still restores, truth still frees, and God is not finished rewriting this story.

A Blessing for the Journey Ahead

Kasey and I want to be clear about what we will always honor, God truly moved among us. In the midst of pain and failure, we stood on holy ground and witnessed the undeniable mercy and power of Jesus Christ. We saw lives saved, prodigals return, families restored, chains broken, and bodies healed. These were not manufactured moments or emotional illusions but were the gracious works of a faithful Savior. Scripture declares, *"Jesus Christ the same yesterday, and to day, and for ever"* **(Hebrews 13:8 KJV)**. God did not move because leadership was perfect but because Jesus is. The miracles were never the fruit of flawless vessels but of hungry hearts and a merciful God who honors faith. As Scripture says, *"The LORD is nigh unto them that are of a broken heart; and saveth such as be of a contrite spirit"* **(Psalm 34:18 KJV)**. Even where people failed, God remained faithful still healing, saving, and pouring out His Spirit. Jesus still heals, restores, and calls people home: *"Come unto me, all ye that labour and are heavy laden, and I will give you rest"* **(Matthew 11:28 KJV)**. No matter what repentance or accountability lies ahead, God's mercy endures, grace restores, and love invites every wounded heart back to Him. For this and all He has done, I will always give Him glory.

A Call to Prayer, Unity, and Compassion

As this book ends, our final call is not towards division but to prayer, unity, and compassion for the entire Body of Christ. Scripture instructs us, *"Brethren, if a man be overtaken in a fault, ye which are spiritual, restore such an one in the spirit of meekness..."* **(Galatians 6:1 KJV)**.

183

Restoration is born from humility and mercy, not anger or resentment. We ask that the kindness of God, not the wrath of man, would lead every heart to repentance and healing, for *"...the goodness of God leadeth thee to repentance"* **(Romans 2:4 KJV)**. We believe God is still at work, restoring, and calling His people back to truth and light. This book is not written to tear down the church but to elevate it. Scripture reminds us that *"For we can do nothing against the truth, but for the truth"* **(2 Corinthians 13:8 KJV)**. Accountability and compassion must walk together. Father has not failed the wounded and weary, *"Jesus Christ the same yesterday, and to day, and for ever"* **(Hebrews 13:8 KJV)**.

As Kasey and I move forward, our choice is to walk in the light God has given us and trust Him with what comes next, believing His promise, *"The LORD is nigh unto them that are of a broken heart..."* **(Psalm 34:18 KJV)**. Whatever paths we take from here, our prayer remains that every heart finds rest in Christ, for He still calls, heals, and restores **(Matthew 11:28 KJV)**. Let love have the final word. Let Christ be glorified in all things.

If *Pulpit of Leaves: Deception in Plain Sight* encouraged you, gave language to something you've carried quietly, or helped restore clarity and hope, we invite you to leave a review on Amazon. Your voice matters. Many others are searching for truth and healing, wondering if they are alone. Even a few honest sentences can help someone else find courage to take their next step. **Scan the QR code below to leave a review on Amazon**

Thank you for being willing to speak. Your voice can make a difference.

Our Next Book is Coming Soon!

UNCHURCHED
Coming Out of Corrupt Systems and Returning to the True Body of Christ

ISBN:9781971163055   **LCCN 2026901456**

What happens when the Church no longer looks like Jesus but still speaks in His name?
Scripture warned us this day would come: a season when Sauls cling to power, Ahabs surrender responsibilities, Jezebels manipulate from behind the throne, false prophets cry *"peace"* where there is none, and wolves learn to preach while wearing shepherds' robes. These are not ancient stories, they are biblical patterns and many believers are living inside them right now. For countless people, the deepest wounds were not inflicted by the world but by the very systems meant to shepherd them. Authority was demanded without accountability. Scripture was twisted to protect leaders and silence pain. Growth was celebrated while sheep were scattered, bruised, and then blamed for bleeding.

Unchurched is a prophetic, pastoral, and unflinching examination of how the Church drifted from the living body Jesus built, into institutional systems. He never designed these systems where control replaces care, loyalty eclipses truth, and obedience to God is quietly redefined as submission to men.

This book is written for the wounded, discerning, and faithful who stayed longer than they should have. *Unchurched* exposes the perversion of spiritual authority, the marketplace gospel, fear-driven giving, and the devastating reality of religious trauma. It confronts the misuse of *"covering,"* the weaponization of Scripture, and the dangerous elevation of loyalty over righteousness while anchoring every claim firmly in the Word of God.

This is not a book about walking away from Christ. It is a book about returning back to Him. Through Scripture and biblical clarity, *Unchurched* guides readers through the wilderness that often follows obedience. This is the place where God heals what systems break, restores identity after misuse, and calls His people out of environments that harm them without calling them away from Himself. It reminds readers that leaving corrupt systems is not apostasy and that separation for obedience has always been part of God's pattern **(Genesis 12:1; Hebrews 13:13)**. For leaders, this book offers a sober warning: *"The shepherds feed themselves... should not the shepherds feed the flock?"* **(Ezekiel 34:2)**. For the silenced, it gives language to pain you were told not to name. For the un-churched but not un-called, it offers hope. God is rebuilding His Church according to His Word, not a brand, platform, or empire, but a living Body led by Christ alone.
Unchurched is not an attack on the Church. It is a call to purity for the Bride of Christ, being sanctified through the washing of the Word and prepared for the return of her Groom.

A Final Word to the Reader
Pulpit of Leaves was written to expose deception, but wisdom required restraint. More than one hundred

pages were intentionally left out. Since this book was written, the Father has continued to move powerfully bringing healing where there was trauma, restoring families that were fractured, rebuilding identity, and revealing just how faithful He is when His people choose obedience. What you have read is only the beginning. If this book opened your eyes, **Unchurched** is where healing takes root and testimony begins. It is an invitation not away from Christ, but deeper into Him, into the restoration of the *"True Body of Christ"* and the gospel of purity, truth, and freedom as God prepares His Bride.

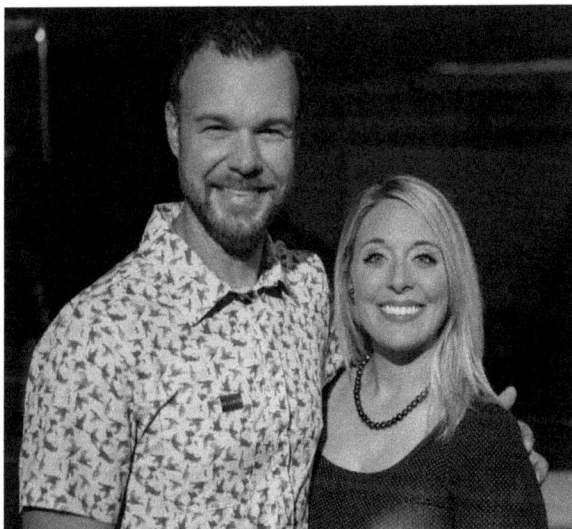

Justin and Kasey Greenwell

Scan the QR code below to find out more about *Unchurched* and walk with us into what the Father is restoring.

www.ingramcontent.com/pod-product-compliance
Lightning Source LLC
Chambersburg PA
CBHW051831090426
42736CB00011B/1742